SECULAR INDIA
Politics of Minorityism

Edited by
RAKESH SINHA

Vitasta

Published by Renu Kaul Verma for
Vitasta Publishing Pvt. Ltd.
4348/4C, Ansari Road, Daryaganj,
New Delhi - 110 002
info@vitastapublishing.com

ISBN 978-93-80828-68-8

First Edition 2012
Second Reprint 2025

MRP ₹ 399

Cover and Layout Design by Vitasta Publishing Pvt. Ltd.
Printed by Thomson Press India Ltd.

Contributors

Rakesh Sinha

Prof Rakesh Sinha is Associate Professor at Delhi University and an Honorary Director of the India Policy Foundation.

Asha Das

Retired as the Secretary of Government of India, Das served as the secretary of the National Commission for Linguistic and Religious Minorities (Ranganath Mishra Commission). Her dissent note to the commission's report led a national debate.

Subramanian Swamy

Janata Party president Dr Subramanian Swamy's political struggles against the Emergency and in exposing the 2G scam are well known. An economist, he was elected Member of Parliament five times and has been a Cabinet Minister also.

Jagdamba Mall

A social activist, Jagdamba specialises on North East, particularly Naga issue.

Meenakshi Lekhi

Supreme Court advocate Meenakashi Lekhi has been a part of the drafting committees on bills like 'Women Reservation Bill' & 'Problem of Sexual Harassment at Workplace' and is chairperson of the Special Task Force on Women Empowerment.

Devang Nanavati

Advocate Devang Nanavati, an expert in international law, is advisor to various government and non-government agencies and is a sports lover heading several sports bodies.

Arif Mohammed Khan

Former Union Minister Arif Mohammed Khan is a well known thinker and politician.

C Issac

History professor C Issac of the Bharatheeya Vichara Kendram has been associated with the ABVP for long and is a regular contributor to *The Organiser*, *Kesari, Vijayavani* and other journals.

Pravin Togadia

Medical professional Dr Pravinbhai Togadia is a working International President of the Vishwa Hindu Parishad.

Bal Apte

Memebr of Rajya Sabha and a senior leader of the BJP.

Shreerang Godbole

A committed RSS functionary and a keen Savarkar researcher, Sreerang Godbole is a diabetes specialist with several books on religion.

Hari S Kartha

Chief Editor of the popular Malayalam daily, *Janmabhumi*.

T N Razdan

Supreme Court lawyer T N Razdan is president of Jammu-Kashmir Vichar Manch.

Vinod K Shukla

Senior Journalist Vinod Shukla, an expert on Uttar Pradesh politics and minority affairs, has worked as reporter and editor with IANS and Sahara Times.

Contents

Acknowledgement xi

Preface xiii

Introduction xvii

1. A Social Philosophy Based On Two Identity Theory 1
   Rakesh Sinha
2. The Shah Bano Effect 15
   Arif Mohammed Khan
3. Beyond Religion and Caste 27
   Asha Das
4. Dimensions of Minority Appeasement 49
   Bal Apte
5. Kerala in the land of Adi Sankara? 61
   C I Issac
6. How Secular is India? 81
   Devang Nanavati

7. Demons Haunt God's Own Country 101
Hari S Kartha

8. Naga Terrorists in League with Politicians 109
Jagdamba Mall

9. Uniform Civil Code: Vote-bank vs National Interest 155
Meenakashi Lekhi

10. Minority Manipulation Virus 165
Dr Pravin Togadia

11. Economic Consequences of Minority Appeasement 173
Subramanian Swamy

12. National Commission for Minorities 197
Shreerang Godbole

13. Appeasement Policy and the Kashmir Crisis 219
T N Razdan

14. UPA's Appeasement of Minorities Debilitating and Dangerous 235
Vinod Shukla

Acknowledgement

This book is a product of a two-day seminar at GLS Campus, Ahmedabad, organized by Bharatiya Vichar Manch (BVM), Gujarat, with Devang Nanavati, a senior lawyer, as coordinator. Heart-felt thanks to BVM and Devang for organizing brilliant presentations that resulted into this book.

I am grateful to Nehru Memorial Museum Library (NMML), India Policy Foundation (IPF) and the cohesive and enthusiastic team of BVM for providing me with all requisite support in editing the book. My special thanks to writers who privileged me with their outstanding contributions. Moreover, it could not have been possible without the generous suggestions and help given by publisher Renu Kaul Verma.

— Rakesh Sinha

Preface

Inspired by Mahatma Gandhi and guided by Pandit Jawaharlal Nehru, along with the founding fathers of our nation, the Constitution of India proclaimed the state neutral in the matters of religion, giving equal rights to every citizen of our nation.

At the time of Independence, we as a nation, accepted secularism as a policy, treating every religion as equal. But, the Government at the helm of affairs implemented matters related to minorities, with total disregard for the very fabric of a secular nation that we Indians opted for. It deliberately followed a minority appeasement policy to safeguard its vote bank. Today appeasement measures have reached such a level that slowly but steadily, we keep chipping away at an already fragile sense of national identity, and thereby erode the 'Bharatiya' value system and ethos, thus threatening the very fundamental that created the structure of our nation.

The Sachar Committee, set up to evaluate the social, economic and educational status of Muslims, in its report in 2006, called for path-breaking efforts to include Muslims in the national mainstream and address perceived inequities experienced by them. It recommended creation of an Equal Opportunity Commission, modelled on the UK Race Relations Act, 1976, to look into the grievances of religious minorities. This fallacious but vicious attempt to equate Race with Religion is now on the anvil, and can only add to inter-community strains.

The Ranganath Mishra Commission, set up to give reservation to the minorities in government jobs and educational institutions, adds to the folly. The Prevention of Communal and Targeted Violence (Access to Justice and Reparations) Bill, 2011, which holds the majority community responsible for all the communal violence in the nation is another example of minority appeasement. That is why it becomes important to have a sincere and honest debate on the Minority-Majority issue.

To discuss the above issues and for giving appropriate directions to the society, the Bharatiya Vichar Manch, an NGO based in Gujarat since the last 20 years, organized a two-day national seminar on "Dimensions of Minority Appeasement" in Ahmedabad. They invited thinkers, social activists and scientists, political workers and people from various walks of life to present their views on the issue, threatening the very base of this secular nation. BVM believes that its combined resources can be utilized to give appropriate direction to our society. The present volume is a result of views expressed by the contributors, during the proceedings of the seminar.

BVM is thankful to Prof Rakesh Sinha, Honorary Director India Policy Foundation, New Delhi, who despite his very tight schedule, accepted our request to edit and compile the work on contemporary issues in the form of a book.

— **Dewang J Aacharya**
Secretary
Bharatiya Vichar Mnach

Introduction

India's biggest challenge in post independent India has been to resurrect its own tradition and values of secularism as a state policy. The history of Indian civilization records an unobstructed growth of diversities of ideas, thoughts, philosophies and spiritual and religious life. Thus, new sects or religion and new interpretation of spiritual life have been accommodated. This is the spirit of evolution of human values, philosophical outlook and spiritual life which forms the core of the Indian variant of secularism.

The mutual respect for each others' feelings, perspectives and aspirations has not deterred dialogue, debate and discourses that at times have even challenge the concepts held by others. It is in this context that politics and the state are expected to remain a neutral spectator in social and spiritual discourses. The social consensus to keep religion out of the political domain helped the Indian civilization to strengthen its commitment to secularism.

Antithetical to this, the western concept of secularism and multiculturalism have been over-occupied with religion. It defines and treats secularism as a political arrangement for coexistence of religions. Such an arrangement evolved through long and multiple religious battles, persecutions and competition sought to hegemonize the state power through numerical strengths of respective religions and turned secularism as guided ideology rather than naturally evolved value of life. Thus, secularism in western society became a pre-condition of civil society where the state defined every religious community on the basis of their respective strengths. The concept of majority and minority became a fundamental ingredient of the western variant of secularism.

Indian Civilisation does not place importance to numerical strength of any sect or religious community. The colonial regime in India, however, used the Semitic parameters to evaluate secularism and introduced the concept of majority and minority in Indian political and social discourse. The colonial state was guided by its political agenda to divide Indian society into religious categories. Their objective was to weaken the nationalist movement and create permanent strife in the society by invoking religious issues. Hindus were defined and projected as 'tyrannical' and 'oppressive' majority and a new minority consciousness was instilled among the Muslims.

The first systematic attack on India's secular world view by the colonial administration was made after the events of 1857. Then Viceroy of India Lord Mayo assigned William Wilson Hunter to find out the answer of the question faced by him: 'Are Mussalmans bound by their religion to rebel against the Queen?'[1] Using statistics

1. F H Skrine, *Life of Sir William Wilson Hunter* (London, 1901) p 199.

provided by the Bengal government, Hunter prepared a report which was later published in the name of "*Indian Mussalmans*" in 1871. Hunter wrote:

> "that our system of public instruction, which has awakened the Hindus from the sleep of centuries, and quickened their inert masses with some of the noble impulses of a nation, is opposed to the traditions, unsuited to the requirements, and hateful to the religion, of the Mussalmans."[2]

In conclusion, he suggested making recommendations along the lines of Mayo's resolution of 7 August 1871 that the government should temper its education system to Muslim requirements. The report communalized the politics and policies and concomitantly, the secular space increasingly squeezed, and communal aspirations and demands were articulated.

Robinson wrote:

> "the effect of the book was considerable, not because it was particularly well argued or well written, but because five weeks after its publication the acting Chief Justice of Bengal was assassinated by a Muslim on the steps of the High Court, and five months afterwards Mayo himself was stabbed to death by a Muslim convict. Thus, Mayo's education measures and Hunter's arguments about Muslim backwardness attained an all-India importance that they did not deserve and might not otherwise have had."[3]

The report recommended separate education and developmental models for Muslims. Many colonial officers, who were trained to

---

2. Hunter, *Indian Mussalmans*, p 168-9
3. Robinson, *Separatism Among Indian Muslims*, Vikas, Delhi 1975, p 104

free education from religious bias, questioned the state policy that favoured traditional education to Muslims. In North West Frontier, New Delhi's demand for special measures for Muslim education was vigorously attacked by the Director of Public Instruction.[4] The officer derided and flawed Hunter's arguments and declared, 'the question of Mahomedan education in India' to have been 'unnecessarily and unfortunately hampered by political considerations.'[5] He was rebuffed by the central colonial administration. The secretary of the local government informed him that "the decadence of Mahomedan scholarship in India, and the disinclination of the Mahomedans, as a body, to fall in with our university system, and the appropriate remedy for these evils, is matters of highest importance, both socially and politically. Socially, because it is a duty incumbent on the British government so to shape its educational measures as to make them agreeable to this large section of the people, who at present by their predilections, or it may be prejudices, are shut out from the influence of our education system. Politically, because the enlightenment of Mussalmans... would prove one of the surest means of attaching them to our rule.[6] It generated a theory of Muslim backwardness and blamed the Hindus for their deprivation and decay.

4. Memorandum by M Kempson, Director Public Instruction , August 1872, NWF Educ, June 1873, IOR(India Office Records)
5. Memorandum by M Kempson, Director Public Instruction , enclosed in Director of P I to secretary to Govt NWF 18 August 1873, NWF Educ, November 1873, IOR (see Robinson, p 105)
6. Secretary to\govt nwf to Director PI , 14 \nove 1873, NWF educ, nove. 1873,ior, robinson, p 105

Thus, the state justified its role as an arbiter between two communities on the question of social, cultural, economic and educational issues. Political considerations made the Muslims a 'favourite' community and it fanned communalization of social and political discourse. Sir John Strachey, who in 1872 officiated as the Governor General, said that Muslims, "constitute a comparatively small but energetic minority of the population whose interests are identical with ours.[7]"

The honorary principal of Calcutta Madrassa, W N Lees, was critical of the government's policy towards Muslims and wrote three strongly-worded letters to *London Times*[8] arguing to abandon the policy of modernization and supported traditional approach of the Indian Muslims. Thus, the liberalism of the West was supplanted by opportunism. The state patronized communal elements, encouraged communal demands and empowered communal organizations. The British policy succeeded in polarising Muslims and in ghettoisation of their mind. It was this divide and rule that was practised till India was partitioned. A section of Indian nationalists countered the British divide-and-rule policy by placating Muslim demands. It legitimized new communal consciousness.

After the independence, the Constituent Assembly took a critical approach to the British policy and definition of secularism, popularized by the colonial theoreticians. It was a self-introspective deliberation and in a way historic. It directed the nation and alerted the contemporary leadership that minorityism was a

7. Quoted by Nursingdas Agarwalla, the *Hindu Muslim Question*, Calcutta, 1951, p 56
8. 14, 20 October, 2 November, 1871

dangerous weapon against the Indian variant of secularism and was anathema to indigenous world view. The emerging idea received support from contemporary intellectuals including Muslim scholars of repute. For instance, Mujeeb argued, "in a state that has declared itself secular, no community should ask for a definition of its status but only assure itself that its identity as a body holding particular beliefs is respected."[9] It was a clear negation of the theory of the existence of minority and majority. The theory of Muslim backwardness was repudiated as a separatist notion. How can a poor Muslim and a poor Hindu be treated differently? The pertinent question emerges, is a Muslim treated discriminately or is he the victim of Hindu majoritarianism? Another related question is has the Indian state pursued communally framed policies to benefit the majority and deprive the minority?

The imaginary allegations against the state and the majority community have been without any evidence. The commissions and committees formed in independent India to probe Muslim backwardness used the Hunter methodology and reinforced backwardness and discrimination theory. The Sachar Committee report is no better than the Hunter Committee report. It communalized the entire political discourse and artificially generated a perception that Muslims were discriminated against. The committee in its probe and investigation could not cite a single example to substantiate its proposition. It was, after all, not the burden of a committee which was asked to placate Muslims by vindicating their leaders' traditional accusation of backwardness and discrimination. The communal perspective of the committee

9. Mujeeb, 554 M Mujeeb, *The Indian Muslims*, London, 1967

left no department or segment of public life untouched from communalization. For instance, Rinchen Dorjee from Arunachal Pradesh Public Service Commission wrote to Sachar on 24 November 2005, "Muslims are free to apply for any post open for all categories.... It may also be kindly noted that the commission does not adopt any application format to indicate religion of the candidate. So there is no occasion to treat the Muslims differently in this state."[10] All state public service commissions were approached with similar demands and apprehensions regarding how many Muslims would have to be selected and discrimination would have to be in force. The committee found no evidence. Nevertheless, the committee concludes that Muslims are discriminated in education, job employment and other public avenues.

The Sachar report is merely a reiteration of ideas propagated by the Muslim elite and the communal leadership. For instance, *The Communalism Combat* wrote, "Indian Muslims are victims of rampant bias in the fields of education, employment, access to credit, poverty level, access to social and physical infrastructure and political representation."[11]

The Sachar Committee report also deliberates on the issue of Muslim representation. Although it was not a part of its terms and conditions, the committee constituted a sub-committee on the demand of the Muslim members of the Sachar Committee and the sub-committee recommended something uncalled for in the secular, democratic politics of independent India. In the

10. Sachar Papers, Public Service Commissions, Vol I Sr NO 33, P. 63, NMML
11. Communalism Combat, January-February 2007, *Sachar ka sach*

following paragraph, the Sachar Committee writes, "on the other hand, the hard fact remains that the percentage of Muslim Members of Parliament and state assemblies/councils is much less at the national and state levels vis-a-vis their proportion in the population."[12] It further states, "taking into account the responses received from those districts which gave complete information, the following tables have been prepared:

(1) Reserved Assembly constituencies which can be de-reserved as the number of Muslim voters in these constituencies varies between 19-46 per cent while the number of SC/ST voters is negligible.

(2) Unreserved Assembly constituencies which can be reserved as the number of SC/ST voters in these constituencies varies between 20-47 per cent while there is no substantial number of Muslim voters.[13]

Thus, it encourages the demand for reservation on the basis of religion and entails an unhealthy competition among political parties. Further, the Ranganath Mishra Commission emboldens such demands. These are structures created by the holders of state power to justify their naked minoritism. Whether the Sachar or Ranganath Mishra Commission demands are met or not, they have become a weapon in the hands of communal organization to consolidate themselves and polarize Muslim masses. Much before the Sachar syndrome, Moin Shakir had warned, "The Muslim political elite appears to be least interested in guiding the community on healthy and secular lines. It does not want to

---

12. Sachar papers, File 86 p 7
13. Ibid. p.10

educate the community in secularism and commitment of modern man to the basic values of democracy and socialism. It is not concerned with science as a 'cultural' discipline with consequence for its outlook, on man and universe. This is why the community is turning to medieval thinking, slogans and solidarity."[14]

The dimension of minorityism has been unleashed to unlimited scale. Its impact is felt not only in political discourse but also at the grass roots level. Two types of bank loans, two variants of scholarships, religious etc increased the communal division. The state has never attempted to know the socio-religious reasons for Muslims remaining backward in comparison to other communities. The present volume is a collection of essays which deals with various dimensions of minorityism practised by the state and the political system.

Devang Nanavati's paper analyses the historical perspective of secularism, particularly in British India. His argument is aptly based on the notion that there is a necessity to make distinction between cultural expression of a nation and the mode of worship of a community. In his compelling presentation, he advocates that culture's inclusiveness should not be perplexed by the majority/ minority syndrome. The definition of a minority group is still vague, without any concrete limiting boundary, and therefore, subjected to the claims of certain religious groups. On the other hand, parallel to the manipulations by the religious groups, vote-hungry political parties also try to swing their agendas in favour of the minorities. The age-old secular tradition of India is, thereby,

14. Moin Shakir, *The Muslim Political Elite in Muslims of India* by Zafar Imam(ed). p 173, Orient Longman, N D, 1975.

rendered porous to this artificially-created anathema.

He concludes, "The Constitution is a transient document and needs to be understood in its spirit, as well as in the context of the times.... The spirit of the Constitution suggests that the religious expression of the majority was already taken for granted and need not be argued at all. Today, however, minority appeasement arising out of the vote-bank politics sidelines the majority population of India and creates a situation which deliberately confuses the cultural expression of Hindus with religious worship."

Arif Mohammad Khan champions the cause of secular polity. In his critically analytical piece, he examines the Shah Bano Case and the role of various institutions. Khan believes that there is need to change the psyche of the people and he attacks narrow-mindedness of any kind. He writes: "The laws made by Parliament could be amended as demanded by the Personal Law Board, but the tone and tenor of the campaign they launched against the Supreme Court judgment caused irreparable damage to the secular fabric of India. I assert that no government can adopt a totally uncompromising attitude, particularly when a section of the people come to nurse apprehensions about their religion. The government must address their concerns. But we must make a distinction between common people and some distant champions of community interests who thrive on slogans like "religion in danger" and the "special identity" of the community. It is prudent to be sensitive to popular will but it is absolutely fatal to lend respectability and credibility to the purveyors of politics of communalism."

Asha Das played a very significant role in the Ranganath Mishra Commission. As a member secretary, she exposed the fact that the Mishra commission was manipulated and its two chapters were changed in an unscheduled meeting. It was widely reported in the media. Her dissent-note created a political debate and exposed the fallacies of the report. In her piece, however, she has not touched at all on such controversies and primarily dealt with the reasons for 'backwardness' and emphasized the need to treat backwardness in a secular manner rather than from religious or communal perspective. She writes, "Backwardness has neither a caste nor a religion. Religion and caste are undoubtedly a part of our present reality. But in consonance with the aims and objectives of the Constitution, it is not for the state to differentiate between its citizens on the basis of caste or religion.

The ostensible reason for special dispensation to minorities is said to be their socio-economically backward status vis-à-vis other categories. The data on literacy, income, life expectancy, IMR etc of minorities, compared to SCs, STs establishes that their status varies from state to state as it is determined by the general state of development prevailing in the area. Their status is generally higher than that of SCs and STs and in most states, compares with that of the other categories, including the Hindus. However, even if they are poorer, the common criterion will enlist all eligible, making separate enumeration redundant."

Bal Apte discusses the growth of the concept of minority and its implications in the country's society and polity. He also found the concept irrelevant in the Indian context. "A deliberate attempt to alienate the Muslim minority from the mainstream has a direct impact in the form of threat of jihadi terror to the civilizations of the world. Ghettoisation, alienation and propagandist education breeds a sense of injury and anger, which finds an outlet that is provided with cool precision. Today, this comes in the form of what can be called the 'cocktail of Koran with Kalashnikov'."

Issac and Hari S Kartha, both deal with the problem of communalism and the response of the state government in Kerala. Issac traces the history of minority appeasement in Kerala and finds the sharp polarization among religious communities was a result of the rat race of votes. The Communists initiated the policy of appeasement and the coalition politics provided respect to it.

The history of minority religious appeasement in Kerala goes back to the days of vote-bank building of the Communist movement.

The major beneficiaries of the Kerala model of coalition politics are the minorities of the Abrahamic religions. The pastoral function of their religious hierarchy enhanced the bargaining capacity of the minorities in the pragmatic politics of Kerala. Above all, these minorities still retain their own political parties. When a coalition ministry is formed, the minority representation in the Cabinet will be much higher than the Hindus because the national parties are forced to accommodate minorities in order to maintain a 'secular' fig-leaf, whereas the constituent partner of the coalition, i.e., the minority-sponsored religious parties secure cabinet berths exclusively for their community. In effect, the equilibrium of the Cabinet always favours the minorities in two ways; viz, prominent portfolios as well as a majority of ministries go to religious minorities.

Take a glaring instance: in the 54 years of the formation of the State of Kerala, who has controlled the portfolio of education? For 25 years, it was under the control of the Muslim League and for another ten years and three months, in the hands of the Catholic-controlled Kerala Congress. National and secular parties could acquire the portfolio only for 18 years and in this duration only four years and three months were the share of a minister with a Hindu name. If this isn't really shocking information to a nationalist, pray, what is?

Hari Kartha concentrates on Muslim communal organizations and the response of the weak political leadership of the state. He writes, "Perhaps nowhere else in India is vote-bank politics as glaring and dangerous as in Kerala. Little wonder that the Muslim League, which was dubbed by late Pundit Jawaharlal Nehru as 'the dead horse' started galloping again in Kerala. This was the result of the Congress and the CPM vying with each other to politically patronize and promote the Muslim League since the sixties. Despite stiff opposition from several quarters, a Muslim majority district of Malappuram was created by E M S Nāmboodiripad when he became chief minister for the second time. Earlier, it was the Muslim communalism of the Muslim League which was the state's bane, today it is the Islamic fundamentalism of the Jamait-e-Islami, the Popular Front and the Peoples Democratic Party that stalks Kerala.

The rudest shock came hardly two months ago when a college professor of a Christian management college was attacked while he was on his way back from church on a Sunday and his right hand chopped off by a gang of Muslim terrorists using an axe in the presence of his sister and aged mother, in broad daylight. The charge against the professor was that he had referred to one Mohammed in a question paper. Making life further miserable for the Professor, the Christian management of the college, as directed by the church diocese, dismissed him from service. The diocese' indirect approval of the barbarous act by the Muslim bigots seems to have more to it than meets the eye. The million-dollar question posed by this twin action is: Are the two minority communities hand-in-glove in Kerala? In the last three years, more than a score of Hindu youths have been killed by the Muslim extremists in different parts of the State. Not only non-Muslims, even a Muslim scholar, Abdul Maoulavi was butchered and buried deep with no trace of them. Kerala, hitherto hailed as 'God's Own Country' is today haunted by demons."

Jagdamba Mall, a social activist, who is known for his work among Nagas, deals with the policy deficit while dealing with the Naga problem and finds that huge amounts of foreign money have been used to fan separatism. Many NGOs have been used as tools to create anti-India feelings. He concludes, "The British rulers first employed Christian missionaries to convert Nagas and then instigated the converted Nagas (Phizo and NNC militants) to start a Middle Age-style inquisition against those Nagas who refused to convert to Christianity and support British policy after 1947. The aim was to establish a 'Christian solidarity' with the US and the UK, with the American and British Baptist Christian Church taking the initiative for the formation of a Christian Sovereign Nagaland. Phizo, who supported the army of Subhash Chandra Bose and fought against the British army, joined the British bandwagon after conversion to Christianity and waged a war on Bharatvarsh to secede from the country and started the Christian inquisitions in support of a Christian crusade to convert all Nagas to please his British masters. Anybody who expressed a different opinion was brutally killed."

Meenakshi Lekhi succinctly discusses the issue of Uniform Civil Code and the failure of the Indian state to treat various religious communities uniformly. The Constitutional provisions and the judiciary's judgment for secularization of the personal laws became the scapegoat of the vote bank politics. She writes,

"The Congress-led UPA and the various Congress State governments themselves have been reassuring the Muslims that government had/has no intention of enforcing a Uniform Civil Code ever since 1938. Unfortunately, even when other parties have come to power in the centre, they have failed to enforce the Uniform Civil Code. This observation is especially relevant when the State of Goa follows the Portuguese code, at par with a Uniform Civil Code and other States have chosen to remain quiet on this issue. In spite of law and order being a State subject and the Supreme Court having given its mandate repeatedly on this issue, one can see through the vote bank politics being employed by various stakeholders."

Pravinbhai Tagodia questions the politics behind the definition of 'minority' and reaches the conclusion that it is the vote bank politics which promotes and patronises communal demands and minority politics. The appeasement, he considers, is a bane for the Indian society and polity. He writes, "The shameless appeasement of the Muslim 'minorities' is done with the sole purpose of garnering their votes. No political party is seen appeasing India's tribes or similar groups, which are the true victims of the industrial age and truly need help. In this process, successive regimes at the centre and the States have kowtowed to an aggressive Islam." He further argues that no division should be made on the basis of religion and favours the concept of One People, One Nation. He says, "The concept of a religious minority should have become a non-issue in Bharat. Instead, the most vocal and organized 'minority' with undeniable extra-territorial loyalty, has been able to become the largest beneficiary group, at the expense of our nation and its long-term interests! What is the real motto of this ultra-vocal 'minority'? Islamic separatism, religious intolerance and anti-nationalism can rightly be called the credo of this 'minority'. Muslim minorities have perfected the art of misusing vote-hungry politician to manipulate, exploit and subvert democratic freedoms. As a result, the virus of Muslim minority manipulation is spreading so rapidly in Bharat that the entire nation is in its grip."

Subramanian Swamy has raised a fundamental question, whether there is any relevance in counting Muslims as 'minority' in the country where they form the second largest population group? In his analytical piece, Swamy critically compares the various majority communities and their roles and argues that application of minoritism in the field of economics is a negation of secularism. He writes, "Minorityism is a recipe for national disintegration and disaster....Muslims and Christians cannot be considered as minorities in Indian society because their disabilities are not an outcome of any deprivation imposed on them. In fact, Muslims and Christians, like the Whites of South Africa, have been the ruling classes in India for a long period. Sequentially, these two religious groups have ruled India for over a thousand years, during which period they practiced religious apartheid against the Hindus. Hence, for the cause of national integrity, patriotic Indians should resist with all their might any attempt to introduce quotas in jobs, education, or for anything else, for the benefit of Muslims and Christians. Those

Muslims and Christians who consider themselves Indians should also, like the Parsis, reject any offer by mischievous politicians to introduce quotas for them. Instead, they should ask for world-class primary and secondary education to empower them to compete on a level playing field with the rest of the society."

Godbole takes a dig at the National Commission for Minorities (NCM) and brilliantly examines its role, functioning and recommendations. The fourth report of the NCM itself recommended abolishing minority quota as it would prove detrimental to the growth of national integration. However, the political leadership of the country has completely ignored it. Godbale writes,

"The NCM has become a Frankenstein's monster out to undermine the Indian state in general and to disempower and emasculate the Hindus in particular. The NCM has been faithfully echoing the demands of powerful fundamentalist Islamic and Christian missionary lobbies. These demands are placed as 'recommendations' to the Central and State governments. For instance,there should be proportionate representation of minorities in the Armed Forces and Police."

TN Razdan deals with the Union Government's policy towards J&K. He finds that the policy has been overloaded with religious consideration, and the politics vitiated the situation. He argues that unlike Sardar Patel, who took bold steps to integrate Hyderabad and suppressed the rebellion of the Nizam, Jawaharlal Nehru was a victim of populism and his approach complicated the problem in Kashmir. He finally concludes, "Kashmir is the worst sufferer of the Congress policies."

Vinod Shukla laboriously collects and analyses statistics related to minority welfare at the central and state level. He finds that huge amount of expenditure has been incurred by the institutions meant for improving the lot of the minority. Many such institutions had been established to placate Muslims. For instance, the U P Minority Financial Development Corporation (UPMFDC) was established in 1984 and after one decade, the National Minorities Development and Finance Corporation was established with a share capital of Rs 500 crore in 1994. In Bihar, the Bihar Awami Cooperative Bank was established in Patna in 1987. The Andhra Pradesh State Minority Finance Commission was established in 1984. After the Sachar Committee report, the budget of such institutions were increased manyfold. Shukla examined the impact of such efforts on secular polity of the country.

The political situation in the country reinforces religion-based politics in the country. There is a need to further examine whether common Hindus or Muslims think in communal terms of sectarianism, or is it imposed by the elite and communal-minded political leadership? Can a secular state sustain plurality and multiculturalism if it is loaded with religious bias, politics and policies? Definitely it is undesirable and dangerous for national unity and integrity. Any policy or institution which creates and promotes two identities must be contested. There is need to further examine why the slogans, premises, demands and nature of minority politics in India reflect continuity and perpetuation of the colonial era.

— Rakesh Sinha

A Social Philosophy Based On Two-Identity Theory

— Rakesh Sinha

What should be the social philosophy of the Indian state? The question is as relevant today in 2012 as it was in 1947. A social philosophy outlines the characteristics of a society that it seeks to build or maintain, and it may be identified by asking, "How does a state look at the various components and sections of its people?" As an example, a colonial state cannot have the same policy as an independent state. While the former would like to treat its people like subjects, the latter treats them as citizens.

During the colonial era, the British tried their best to destroy the unity, harmony and goodwill among the people of India. Their philosophy has been characterized as a policy of 'Divide and Rule'. The operative part of their philosophy was to locate 'identities' within the country, strengthen them and to encourage unhealthy and bitter competition between them, in order to divide them. They found the social liberalism, cultural openness and philosophical superiority of Indian civilization and people as the stumbling block in their plan and, therefore, created differences among the people on the basis of attire, language, caste and religion. Their sole objective was to weaken Indian nationalism. They succeeded in at least one field–creating differences and unhealthy rivalry among identities on the basis of religion. The formation of the Muslim League in 1906 was a result of this philosophy, the conspiracy taking a concrete shape. They wanted Muslims and Hindus as two separate, rival sects in opposite camps.

A long exercise for dividing the people into two artificial groups as majority and minority continued for the next forty years. This division they sought was unnatural because both the communities had a long history of harmony as well as struggle against each other which turned their relationship a symbiotic one. The aliens found that the job was not easy and hence their strategists chose to communalise the economic base of the Indian society. The first stone towards realizing this goal was laid by instituting the Hunter Committee. In his report of 1870, based on a study conducted just in Bengal, William Wilson Hunter, an ICS and the editor of Bengal Gazette, blamed the colonial state and the majority community, the Hindus, for the backwardness of the Muslims. The committee reached this conclusion on the basis of statistics provided by the Government. It was the first systematic attempt to theorise the majority–minority dictum on the soci-economic plank. This report provided the legal, constitutional and ethical grounds for the creation of a policy to privilege Muslims economically and politically. The Muslim leadership, thus, discovered a right to organize themselves socially and politically, playing the minority card.

There is also another dimension to this. The Muslims were,

in a way, convinced that they were a minority and they started comparing their illiteracy, unemployment and poverty to those of the Hindus. In other words, minoritism started taking priority over the feeling of being equal citizens. This minority philosophy and thought finally became the basis of the two-nation theory.

The seeds of the demand for Pakistan were, therefore, sown by the Hunter Committee report. The report wasused as a tool by the fundamentalist forces to create cleavage between Hindus and Muslims. It had been reprinted in the 40s in Urdu and English and proved more popular than its earlier edition.

II

After the partition of India, the Constituent Assembly took an unbiased and critical decision about the social philosophy of the state. This related to the relevance, practicality and compulsions of adopting or discarding the colonial social system. The committee that was set up to consider the rights of the minorities was headed by Sardar Vallabhbhai Patel. Its report was discussed in the Constituent Assembly. Tajamul Hussain, a prominent member of the minority community, pointedly asked the majority community, "Will you allow us to stand on our feet? Will you allow us to remain a part of the Indian society? Do you regard us as equal partners? Will you allow us to march shoulder-to-shoulder with you? Do you want us to be partners in joy and grief? If yes, please stop talking about providing protection or reservation to us. We want to stand on our own feet. If we stand on our feet, we will not have an inferiority complex. We are not inferior in any way. We are not different from you in any way. Yes, we have a different way of praying to the Almighty, but tagging us as minority merely on this ground is not fair. The minorities were created by the British and that concept has also gone away with them. Please remove this word from your dictionary now. There is no minority in India now. These sections existed only till there were separate electoral systems and separate reservation of posts for both communities but now, all that is over and all have merged into one community."[1]

Tajamul Hussain was not alone. Begum Aijaj Rasul and Dr HC Mukherjee (a Christian) also considered majority and minority categorization as dangerous for communal harmony and unity of the country. Rasool had said in her speech, "Those Muslims who wanted to go to Pakistan have already left. Those who decided to stay back want to live here on friendly terms with the majority and would like to mould themselves according to the times and the society. I am not saying they have to change themselves according to the wishes of the people of the country, but I also do not want any bias or discrimination against us. That is why I say that being citizens of this great country, we are equal partners in the hopes and aspirations of the people."

As a result of these discussions, two kinds of consensus emerged: One, there would be common citizenship in the country and every citizen will have equal rights and duties. The basis of this common citizenship would not merely be Geographical location and constitutional-political criteria. As Rasul had said, the decision of those who decided to stay back should not be considered as having been taken merely on the basis of geographical boundaries, but a considered decision to live in a spirit of harmony, taken on the basis of history, traditions and philosophical understanding. Possibly, Pandit Jawaharlal Nehru had talked about the same understanding in the form of questions before Muslim intellectuals. Addressing a convocation at the Aligarh Muslim University, he had told the majority Muslim audience, "I have said that I am proud of my heritage and my ancestors who provided an intellectual and cultural foundation to the country. How do you feel about this past? Do you also feel part of this tradition and heritage? Like me, do you also feel proud of this heritage? Or do you feel alienated and withdraw yourself without having experienced this great feeling of being the owner of this rich treasure house of heritage? I am asking this question because in recent years, many forces have been trying to give a distorted and biased twist to history. You are Muslims and I am a Hindu. We may have separate religious faiths or we may be atheists but this cannot take away the common cultural heritage that binds both of us. When the past has kept us united, how can the present and the future divide our souls?"[2]

Genesis of India's nationalism is not limited to 1957 or 1857. The history, culture, philosophy, national personality and traditions of India before the onset of Islam, complete, enliven and strengthen the national character of India. We cannot talk about India's nationalism, unity and harmony by ignoring this rich heritage.

The second consensus that emerged was that there would be a rule of law in the country. Rule of law means that everyone will be equal in the eyes of law. The law will not discriminate between the people. Institutions and policies are created in the country on the basis of law.

III

In the formative years of Independence, India countered the Pakistani propaganda at the global level by telling the world that there was no discrimination against Muslims in India on social or political grounds; that Hindus were being victimized in Pakistan but India was being accused of mistreating its minorities. India not only accepted those Muslims who were supporters of the two-nation theory but also those who had accepted the citizenship of Pakistan. There were 18,000 railway employees who had taken up Pakistani citizenship but later opted for India. "The Government of India took back Muslim officers and employees and re-appointed them."[3]

At that time, the government Publication Department published many documents to counter Pakistani propaganda that Muslims were discriminated in India.[4]

The Constituent Assembly did not feel the need to use words like *panth nirpeksh* or secularism in the Constitution. It is not difficult to guess the reason for this. The social philosophy of any state largely depends on the world view of the majority community. Even after the tragedy of the partition, if the Indian state could not discriminate against the people on the basis of religion or race, nor the demand for exchange of population was made, it was due to Hindus' deep conviction in secularism and multicultural values. In other words, the philosophy of the historic community of a nation reflects the philosophy of the state. If society cannot tolerate multipolarity of faiths for a long time historically and philosophically, it cannot remain secular for long. The European countries are an example of this. Many of these countries have declared multicultural identity as impractical after the increasing Jihadi incidents. Belgium, France, Italy and Australia have either banned the burqa or there is a growing demand in those countries to ban it. In fact, the Belgium senate in 2010 has passed a resolution to this effect by a majority of 134 out of 136 members. Two members were absent.

The message is clear. The multi-polarity propagated by Christian societies was a temporary and romantic philosophy which could not stand the test of time.

India, despite its ups and downs, has managed to maintain its multi-polarity. That is why, when in 1976, the Government added the word secularism to the Constitution through the 42nd Constitution Amendment Bill there was neither much reaction nor protest.

A canard is being spread that Muslims are being discriminated against in India. Where and how? Neither can the Muslim intellectuals nor the power-hungry politicians prove this. The Hunter Commission report has been revived. It is not a crime to study the Socio-economic condition of Muslims, but this was done to establish a new identity with an ulterior motive. The population of Hindus in Pakistan and Bangladesh reduced to negligible. According to the 2001 Census, the rate of growth of Muslims in India has been more than that of the average growth rate of India. While the national rate of growth between 1961 and 2001 has been 134 per cent, the growth of Muslims has been 194 per cent. Almost in all the States, the growth of the Muslim population has been higher than that of the average population growth cutting across religions. Some figures given below prove this.

Population Growth Rate: 1961-2001

State	Average of all Religions	Muslim
Kerala	88.4	159.7
Uttar Pradesh	136.9	194.3
Bihar	136.1	201
Assam	140.1	200.5

State	Average of all Religions	Muslim
Maharashtra	144.9	238.5
Gujarat	145.6	163.2
Haryana	178.6	321.1
Delhi	421	944

A section of Muslim intellectuals and communal organizations have been leveling imaginary and cooked-up charges of discrimination against Hindus. The myth of discrimination was institutionalized by the competitive power politics. The state and politics based on Nehruvian model States, instead of countering these allegations, have been patronizing them. In other words, the social philosophy invented by the colonial administration has been re-established in India. The Muslims had been calling themselves backwards in pre 1947 era and they feel the same even today. It was this argument of backwardness, discrimination and Hindu domination that led to the demand for Pakistan in 1947. The duty of the state was to find out the true reasons for their backwardness: whether the burden of medieval thinking and religion did not allow them to go along with the mainstream and modernity, deter to change. Were they illiterate because of lack of schools and colleges, or did they lag behind due to their attitude towards education? Their bank accounts were not less, not because the banks were not allowing them to open accounts but because of the interest on money, *Riba* (Islam is against taking or giving interest). These issues should have been debated at social and political levels but instead, Nehruvian and Marxist intellectuals kept Muslims insulated from the intervention of the state, independent research and critical opinion.

When the Hindu Code Bill was being debated in the

1950s, during the debate in the Lok Sabha N C Chatterjee asked passionately, "Why are the changes in personal laws being limited only to Hindu society? Is this not a communal provision that defies the basic directives of the Constitution? The Constitution talks about a common civil code for all citizens."[5]

Smith has quoted the leader of the Praja Socialist Party, Acharya Kripalani. Taking part in the debate on the Hindu Marriage Act, he had said, "If we claim to be a democratic nation, I would say that laws should be made not for one community but for the entire country. Today, the Hindus are not mentally prepared to accept the laws of *talaq* just as the Muslims are opposed to the laws for a single marriage. Will the Government introduce a law for a single marriage for Muslims? Will our Honourable Law Minister implement the single marriage rule for all communities? I would say that is the democratic process, and the other method is communal. It is not only the Hindu Mahasabha that is communal; the Government is also communal, whatever it might claim."[6]

The Indian state has never tried to tell the Muslims to accept social, educational and cultural reforms. The Muslim intellectuals, who were educated in the modern system, restricted these for themselves. They termed this attitude of the Government towards Muslims as positive, secure and loving. The convent-educated Muslims never allowed the other Muslims to come out of the Madarsas. Their viewpoint was decided by Madarsas, Masjids and Marxists. The state encouraged them to live according to Islamic laws. They were given Constitutional rights to live as a special community. This was the beginning of the 'appeasement policy'.

At the same time, questions about education and poverty were also being raised in different quarters. But instead of tackling these issues through education, communal solutions were sought to be imposed. This was the second stage of appeasement. In 1957 a sub-committee was set up to look into the complaints of Muslims. After this came demands for reservation for Muslims in jobs, education and economic activities. The basis for this was the same which was raised by the Muslim League before Partition i.e. discrimination against Muslims. Humayun Kabir wrote,[7] "We have all heard and read in newspapers that there is discrimination in jobs and appointments while the Constitution talks about equal opportunities and fair selections. Why is this so? When the jobs are few and candidates are more, the employer will have the option to select and reject. He could take decisions on the basis of family connections, region or religion. The primary reason for this is lack of job opportunities. This will affect those more that need the jobs. Hindus will complain against Hindus, Muslims will complain against Muslims and Hindus will also complain against Muslims while Muslims will complain against Hindus. But the basic cause is lack of resources."

However, Muslims rejected the arguments of senior intellectuals like Humayun Kabir, AAA Faizi, Moin Shakir, M Mujib, M C Chagla and Arif Mohammad Khan and accepted activist Muslim intellectuals like Javed Anand, Teesta Setalvad, Syed Shahabuddin and Aziz Burney as their spokespersons because they spoke their language. The Indian state also started side-lining the top ranking intellectuals and involving activist intellectuals in its decision-making process. Hamid Dalvi writes, "The old Muslim habit of blaming the Hindus for their problems reappeared and was set more firmly than ever.... Muslims remained backward because there were religion-bound revivalists who refused to modernize themselves."[8]

The state went on appeasing the Muslims and their demands kept on increasing. And soon the state started following totally communal policies. Food, employment and policies were decided on communal terms. Gopal Krishna wrote, "Muslims have started understanding the critical importance of the state."[9]

In the '80s as the role of mass vote banks became vital, the policy of Muslim appeasement became more pronounced. In 1983, a 15-point programme was announced by the Prime Minister which was basically a programme for Muslims. The 8th, 9th and 10th points of this programme specifically mention that priority in jobs in the security forces of the Centre and States, police, railways, nationalised banks and public-sector undertakings would be given to Muslims. In 1985, Rajiv Gandhi declared, "It is imperative to improve the condition of the minorities to strengthen the social fabric of the country". And in 2005, Manmohan Singh announced that, "the minorities had the first right on the resources of the country." Had he stated that the poor and the deprived had the first right over the resources, it would have been a secular statement. Justice VR Krishna Iyer has rightly stated in the context of the minorities that a tag of minority cannot be a justification to loot the resources of the country.

But the Indian state has made minoritism the focus of its policies. The Gopal Singh Committee (1983), the Sachar Committee (2005) and the Ranganath Mishra Commission (2007) were three important committees that were specifically set up to look into the economic, educational and social problems of minorities. But all the committees used only colonial vocabulary, quotations and statements to propound their case. The committees and their reports have not been able to establish or substantiate a single instance of discrimination against the minorities. But they kept on repeating that Muslims were backward, illiterate and deprived and it was the state and the majority community which were responsible for this. Once again, special economic, educational and social policies are being implemented especially for them. On the lines of colonialism, demands are being raised for reservation for Muslims in education, jobs and in the Assemblies.

The consensus that had been worked out in the Constituent Assembly has been totally demolished by minoritism and its policies. Justice VR Krishna Iyer wrote in the Frontline magazine (November, 2006) that, "The provision to treat the Minority as favoured category is not to hold them as privileged class over the Majority...the nation is one and the minority and weaker sections just a part of it, the minority is not a superior nation in the republic."

The Allahabad High Court had ruled that it was wrong to regard Muslims as minority. This verdict of 5 April, 2007 came as a deadly blow to the Muslims.

Those who control the state today have a limited vision and narrow minds, but unlimited ambition. That is why the present and the future of the country are not significant for them. And, therefore, the policy of appeasement they eventually follow is adversely affecting the interests of villages, kasbas, the deprived, Scheduled Castes and Scheduled Tribes. The recommendations of the Sachar Committee and the Ranganath Mishra Commission prove this. Ironically, some members of the Ranganath Mishra Commission illegitimately changed the report and the member secretary Asha Das was kept in the dark which led her to write a dissent note. The state has created structures like the

National Commission for Minorities (NCM), and various other commissions and committees to ensure that the secularist social philosophy survives and to garner support base on the basis of religion and sects. It has dangerous consequences. The secular mode of developments and holistic approach has been destroyed by the communal politics. Omar Khalidi's statement in this context is very relevant:

"Whatever political measures the state needs to take at the Central and State levels for the Muslims must not be at the expense of the rest of the people, of other religious faiths. Muslims' economic interest is not in competition with or at the expense of other classes of Indians. Plans for improvement of the economic condition of Muslims can only be part of the general programme of poverty alleviation meant for all. The state will need to formulate and implement programmes in a manner that it will not be seen as appeasement of minorities."[10]

A distorted vision of social philosophy sees poverty, unemployment and even crime from a communal angle. This may give instant benefit in the form of vote banks, but in the long run, it shatters national unity.

An alternative vision for the Indian state needs to be evolved based on harmonious development of all the limbs of the society and nation. The warning by Dr H C Mukherjee echoes in our ears. He had aptly stated in the Constituent Assembly that we cannot take a risk of accepting any community as minority, based on religion. He further observed that such thing would endanger the unity and integrity of India. The present political establishment and politics hardly care for the sane advice and wisdom of the Constituent Assembly. Their vote bank mission does not allow them to think in terms of the welfare of the nation. Any ideology which plays the subversive role on our secular democracy should be defeated.

References

1. Indian Constituent Assembly, 26 May, 1949, p 515, Vol-VIII, (a) Lok Sabha Secretariat, 1994
2. Speech in Aligarh Muslim University, 24 January 1948
3. *India's Minorities*, Publication Department, Information & Broadcasting Ministry, Old Secretariat, Delhi. 1948, p 25
4. *Muslims in India*, First Edition, 1952, Second 1964, Third 1966
5. Lok Sabha debate, 1955, Part-II, Section- 4, Column-7376
6. Smith DE, *India Is a Secular State*, 1963, p 286
7. *Muslims in India*, Publishing Division, Government of India. p 6.
8. *Muslim Politics in India*, Nachiketa Publication, Mumbai, 1968. p 32-33
9. Ed Madan T N, *Piety and Politics of Indian Muslims in Muslim Community of South Asia: Culture and Society*, Manohar 1995.
10. Khalidi Omar, *Muslims in Indian Economy, Three Essays*, Guruwang, 2006, p 227

The Shah Bano Effect

— Arif Mohammed Khan

The Supreme Court judgment in the Shah Bano case was delivered in response to an appeal, arising out of an application filed for maintenance by a divorced Muslim woman under Section 125 of the Code of Criminal Procedure.

The facts of the case are that one Mohd Ahmed Khan, an advocate by profession, was married to Shah Bano Begum in 1932. Three sons and two daughters were born of that marriage. In 1975, the wife was thrown out of her matrimonial home by her husband. In April 1978, she filed a petition under Section 125 in the court of judicial magistrate, asking for maintenance at the rate of Rs 500 per month. On 6 November 1978, the husband pronounced an irrevocable divorce on his wife. The line of defence he adopted was that the woman (Shah Bano) had ceased to be his wife and he was under no obligation to pay her any maintenance. In August 1979, the court directed the husband to pay a sum of

Rs 25 per month. In July 1980, in a revised application, the High Court of Madhya Pradesh enhanced the amount of maintenance to Rs 179.20 per month. The husband filed an appeal against the Madhya Pradesh High Court in the Supreme Court.

Under Section 125 (1) (a), a person, who, having sufficient means, neglects or refuses to maintain his wife, who is unable to maintain herself, can be asked by the court to pay a monthly maintenance to her at a rate not exceeding 500 rupees per month. By clause (b) of the Explanation to Section 125 (1), the definition of a wife covers a divorced woman who has not remarried.

This particular provision is part of the country's criminal law, aimed at prevention of vagrancy and destitution. It has nothing to do either with the personal laws of various communities, or the religious faith of the spouses. It is uniformly applicable to all citizens of India. The Section 125 was enacted to provide a quick and summary remedy to a class of persons who are unable to maintain themselves. Neglect by a person of sufficient means to maintain them and the inability of these persons to maintain themselves are the objective criteria which determine the applicability of Section 125. This is a measure that intends to serve a social purpose, cutting across the barriers of religion. This provision was not designed to supplant the religion of the litigant parties or their personal laws, if these were to affect the applicability of this provision.

In my speech in the Lok Sabha, I had submitted that Section 125 is a provision of criminal law; it is rooted in the theory of social justice and has no relationship with personal law, which is essentially a civil law. Section 125 provides for quick and summary remedy to persons unable to maintain themselves. The provision does not deal with the rights of a married or divorced woman, but is meant to provide bare minimum relief to those who do not possess sufficient means to keep their body and soul together.

Secondly, the law does not become operative automatically on divorce. It can be invoked by a destitute divorced woman, who, if she feels that such remedy is prohibited by religion, can choose not to avail it. But most women who seek relief under Section 125 are those who are divorced through the instrumentality of triple divorce i.e. three pronouncements in one sitting. Admittedly, this method of divorce is hostile to the provisions of the *Quran* and even the law, as practised in India, describes it as 'good in law and bad in religion'. Why is it that Muslim Personal Law Board was so upset over the provision of so paltry a sum to a destitute woman but feels no hurt when men resort to a divorce that militates both against the *Quran* as well as religious morality?

Tirmidi reports that when the Holy Prophet was informed about a man who had divorced his wife by three pronouncements, he stood up in anger and said: "You are playing sport with the book of God, while I am among you." Possibly it was this anger that made Caliph Umar whip men who resorted to triple divorce. I had argued that today such physical punishment is not possible, so there should be financial liabilities imposed, to deter men from making three pronouncements in one sitting.

The objective of Section 125 is to prevent social vagrancy and destitution. The law takes the view that no person, man or woman, in the absence of necessary wherewithal to live, is going to lie down and wait for death. In this situation, he or she is likely to commit acts that may be injurious to the health of the society and the person concerned. Ideally, it is the obligation of the government to ensure that no one suffers on account of non-availability of food but due to constraint on resources, the law attempted to find alternative sources. In 1975, when the Criminal Procedure Code was revised, the responsibility, in the case of divorced women, was shifted to their former husbands.

Even if we accept the viewpoint of the Personal Law Board that after divorce, the husband and wife become strangers and no liability devolves on the former husband, nothing prevents him from doing charity to a destitute stranger, who also happens to be his former wife. Maulana Abdul Majid Daryabadi commenting on the phrase "and do not forget grace among yourselves" that appears in verse 2.237, says that the exhortation is that "even on the occasion of divorce which announces annulment of the relationship, do not refrain from showing goodness, consideration and concession."

Moreover, Section 125 deals with a situation where the needy persons are placed in an exigent condition (*Iztarari Halat*) and the Islamic law permits such persons to consume the prohibited to save their lives without incurring any liability. Syed Qutub in his book, *Islam the Misunderstood Religion,* has narrated an interesting episode that shows the importance attached to the sanctity of human life and body:

> "It was reported to Caliph Umar that some boys in the service of Hatib Ibn Abi Balta'a had stolen the she-camel of a man from the tribe of Muznah. When Umar questioned the boys they admitted the theft, and he ordered their hands to be chopped off. But

> on second thoughts, he said, "By God I would cut their hands if I did not know that you employ these boys and starve them so that they would be permitted to eat, that which is prohibited unto them."

Then he addressed their employer saying:

> "By God, since I have not cut their hands, I am going to penalize you with a fine that shall pain you" and ordered the latter to pay double the price of the she-camel.

Here the thieves were pardoned because they were starving and a fine was imposed on the employer who did not provide them adequate remuneration to take care of their needs.

Basically, my arguments were based on my understanding that Islam is not only an inherited culture or a set of legal and social values. It is a creed or thought that seeks to transform the soul. It is a religion of *Taqwa* (God consciousness) and not *Fatwa* (Legalistic Quiddities). The laws derived from the *Quran* and Prophetic traditions are sensitive to the context and have the dynamism, to respond to the demands of the time and the place in which they are applied. Moreover, the underlying theme of Islamic teachings is 'excellence of conduct'. It is reported that when the Prophet arrived at Medina, he repeatedly exhorted his audience with the following lines:

> "O People spread peace, feed the hungry, do your duty to your kin, prostrate in the nights when others are sleeping and enter paradise in comfort."

While concluding my speech, I had said that the laws made by parliament could be amended as demanded by the Personal Law Board, but the tone and tenor of the campaign they had launched against the Supreme Court judgment would cause irreparable damage to the secular fabric of India. Later, I repeatedly asserted that no government can adopt a totally uncompromising attitude (particularly when a section of the people come to nurse apprehensions about their religion) and must address their concerns. But we must make a distinction between common people and some distant champions of community interests who thrive on slogans like "religion in danger" and the "special identity" of the community. It is prudent to be sensitive to popular will but it is absolutely fatal to lend respectability and credibility to the purveyors of politics of communalism.

The apprehension I had expressed became a reality even before the Bill to undo the effect of the Supreme Court judgment was introduced in Parliament. In the second week of January 1986, Prime Minister Rajiv Gandhi announced his decision to accept the demand of the Personal Law Board. The backlash it aroused was so severe that the government felt the need to "do something" to divert public attention. Ayodhya came in as a handy expedient.

The locks in Ayodhya were opened on 1 February 1986. I met Rajiv Gandhi at his office on 6 February and gave my assessment of the situation. I said that the Shah Bano issue would be relegated to the background and Ayodhya would become the new ground of agitation. The Prime Minister told me that he had no such apprehension as he had informed the parties concerned before the locks were opened. He was confident but I had my doubts, though the subsequent silence of the Personal Law Board over Ayodhya proved that Rajiv Gandhi's early confidence was perhaps not out of place. In fact, the Chairman of the Personal

Law Board, Maulana Abul Hasan Ali Nadwi, used strong words to denounce the Babri Masjid Movement. In his autobiography '*Karavane Hayat*', Maulana writes:

> "The author (like many other people of vision) saw with open eyes that the manner in which Babri Masjid movement was conducted, generated such tremendous enthusiasm in the minds of the majority for Hindu revivalism that even great Hindu religious leaders had not been able to arouse. From the Islamic viewpoint, it was sheer lack of foresight, narrow-mindedness and from the viewpoint of a religious community, it was like committing collective suicide."[1]

It clearly appeared to be a deal. A legislation on one hand, to undo the Supreme Court judgment which was viewed by Personal Law Board and their camp followers in Congress as a threat to a distinct and separate Muslim identity and opening of the temple gates at Ayodhya on the other, to mollify Hindu sentiment aroused because of the fresh attempts to revive the "special identity theory" associated with Muslim League politics and partition of the country. This was the supposed "balance".

The fallout of Shah Bano and Ayodhya is part of our history. Arguably, after the Partition of India, no other decision has generated so much communal hatred and violence. The country has paid a heavy price and machinations adopted in 1986 predictably failed to yield desired results. On one hand, Ayodhya continues to stir passions and we are nowhere near a solution. On the other hand, the Supreme Court's interpretation of the Muslim Women Act passed in 1986 has created fresh discontent among the ranks of the Personal Law Board and their likes.

The Personal Law Board had asserted with great vehemence that a Muslim husband has no liability beyond the *Iddat*, i.e., a period of three months after divorce. They had not merely endorsed, but were actually involved with the drafting of the Muslim Women (Protection of Rights on Divorce) Bill 1986 to give effect to their standpoint. However, the Supreme Court in its judgment had held that "nowhere has Parliament provided that reasonable and fair provision and maintenance is limited only to the *Iddat* period and not beyond it. It would extend to the whole life of the divorced wife unless she gets married for a second time." The Court restored to divorced Muslim women what the government, at the instance of the Personal Law Board, had denied them.

The result was obvious. Then Chairman of the Personal Law Board, Abul Hasan Ali Nadwi, in a presidential address at the Kanpur Convention in 1989 observed: "The historic rather history making movement of Muslims to secure the Muslim Women Bill in 1986, appears to have been an exercise in futility, rather it can be likened to "*Koh Kandan Kaah Bar Awardan*" (we dug a mountain only to find a molehill)."[2]

It is ironical that the then chairman of the Personal Law Board indulged in such harsh indictment of a legislation, in whose drafting, he and his colleagues in the Personal Law Board had actively participated. This is no surmise; Abul Hasan Ali Nadwi in his autobiography, *Karavan-e-Zindagi*[3] has written:

> "We met the Prime Minister again on 17 February 1986. Maulana Minnatullah Rahmani (general secretary Personal Law Board) was also present on this occasion. Ashok Sen, the Law

> Minister who was sitting in the waiting room, told me: "Maulana Saheb, we have received many letters from Muslim judges and legal experts supporting the judgment of the Supreme Court, but the majority of the Muslims are with you...." The Prime Minister himself came and escorted us to the meeting room. On his asking, the Law Minister took out a three-page draft and started reading it clause by clause. It took three hours to read these three pages. It was a matter of satisfaction and pleasure that the Prime Minister raised questions about every clause and suggested how it should be worded. We observed his unusual interest in this matter and felt that he had made some advance preparations. On each clause he would solicit our views and give instructions to the Law Minister accordingly."

On page 135 of the same volume, he records:

> "At the instance of the Prime Minister, a meeting was held at the residence of Mrs Najma Heptullah, the Deputy Chairman of Rajya Sabha, attended by prominent Muslim MPs, Law Minister Ashok Sen, State Minister HR Bhardwaj and we (MPLB members). This meeting considered the possible difficulties that may arise in the enforcement of the proposed bill. One of the questions raised was regarding the maintenance of a divorced woman, who has no surviving blood relations to take care of her. We responded that in that case, the responsibility can be given to the state Waqf Boards. This satisfied everybody."

It is important to remember that the Supreme Court in its judgment had highlighted the secular nature of Section 125 of the Criminal Procedure Code, but at the same time had relied on a verse from the *Quran* showing that the scripture itself provides for reasonable and fair maintenance to be paid to a divorced woman. The Personal Law Board objected to the judgment on two grounds. Firstly, it had interfered in Muslim Personal Law and secondly, it tried to interpret the holy scripture without any right to do so. But they conceded that it was Yunus Saleem, the Counsel for the Personal Law Board who had drawn the attention of the court to the Quranic verse in support of his plea that the Muslim divorced women have adequate protection and therefore, should be excluded from the purview of Section 125. It appears that the court found this argument supportive of Section 125 and they used it to show that any provision for a divorced woman is not against the teachings of Islam.

This line of argument is supported by many classical jurists of Islam. During the height of the controversy in 1985, Professor Rafiullah Shihab wrote a lengthy article in *Pakistan Times* saying that according to a principle laid down by the Hanafi jurists, "If a husband does not maintain his wife properly, she can get her maintenance allowance fixed through a court. This fixed maintenance allowance will not only be paid to her as a wife but also after divorce." Then he quotes Allama Najeem, a famous jurist, who has discussed this issue in his book *Al-Bahr Al-Raiq*. Allama Najeem says that on this issue there is a difference of opinion among the jurists. According to Imam Muhammad, the husband is not required to pay maintenance to his divorced wife while the more famous Imam Abu Yusuf thought differently. He felt that a husband will have to pay this amount even after divorcing his wife. Allama Najeem, after quoting these mutually conflicting reports, holds that the argument for stopping the wife's maintenance allowance after divorce is weak. He agrees with jurists who hold that a woman, not maintained properly, can knock at the door of a court and get her maintenance allowance fixed. The husband is bound to pay this amount regularly. If he refuses to do so, he should be put behind bars. If it would have been possible for the husband to save his skin by divorcing his wife, he would have preferred to do so. But Islamic law does not allow him to do so. He will have to pay this amount even after divorcing her."[4]

Imam Hasan Basri, a famous theologian of the first Islamic century also held that "there is no time limit regarding payment of maintenance. It should be paid according to one's capacity."[5]

Sheikh Mustafa as-Sabaee, a prominent theologian associated with Ikhwan, commenting upon a proposed Syrian law that provided for maintenance to divorced woman for a period of two years after divorce, observed: "If the divorced woman is of marriageable age, maintenance should be paid till her remarriage; if she is old she should be paid till her death."

Surely, the leaders of the Personal Law Board were not unaware of these juristic opinions. Yet they raised the cry of "Islam and its religious laws in danger." They saw in this as an opportunity to resurrect the old politics of religious identity and arrogate themselves to the status of the sole spokesmen of the community. Unfortunately, the government succumbed to their pressure and agreed to adopt a legislation that would render the Supreme Court judgment ineffective. This action led to a chain of events that resulted in the revival of the dead horse of communal and separatist politics. How deeply our national ethos was affected by this sordid drama can be understood from the fact that even now, that is, after more than two and half decades of its enactment, we still continue to discuss and endure its baleful effects.

References

1. Maulana *Karavane Hayat*, Vol 4 p 130
2. Tamire Hayat, *Organ of Nadwa* 25 May 1989
3. *Karavan-e-Zindagi*, Vol 3 p133
4. *Al-Bahr Al-Raiq* Vol VI p 189-190
5. *Muhalla Ibn Hazm* Vol 10, p 248

Beyond Religion and Caste

—Asha Das

In common parlance, when we talk of 'appeasement', it means we are placating someone by acceding to their demands or by favouring them. Demands are generally made by or on behalf of those categories of the community, who feel they have been or are being denied benefits available to the better-off members of the community. Acceding to the demands need not necessarily be indicative of 'appeasement'. Demands are often accepted where it is perceived that injustice has been done. Appeasement implies favouring for a favour in return. Appeasement connotes acceding to demands or suo motto granting concessions or favours in the hope of getting support and goodwill. It does not, therefore, always reflect a rational, just or equitable decision.

There is a need to debate the growing perception, that in this country, which is home to many religions and castes, the governments of our secular state are following policies which favour certain castes or creeds on the basis of criterion which are discriminatory and not universally applied to all its citizens. The belief is that this is being done for extraneous considerations to gain advantages for political and other ends at the cost of other communities. Amongst others, the reasons for this view can be ascribed to the following:

1. The fact that the government, in its wisdom, has decided to overlook the considered view taken by the framers of our Constitution that the government policies and programmes will not discriminate on the basis of caste, religion, sex or creed. This has strengthened the belief that the policy of minority appeasement is being followed. The number of people in the country, who believe this, is growing and is therefore, a cause for worry.
2. Some decisions taken in the past and recent initiatives taken by the government have substantially contributed to this. Special consideration to Muslims for religious pilgrimages, identification of minority districts and special dispensation to them in terms of legal, educational and other benefits, appointment of committees such as the Sachar Committee and Ranganath Mishra Commission etc, have brought to fore the discriminatory treatment provided/proposed on religious ground.
3. The number of castes, classes and religious communities who are becoming entitled to special programmes and affirmative action by the State is growing thus increasing a sense of deprivation amongst the poor and deserving backwards.
4. Even if we believe that the benefits are to be given to those amongst the minorities who are deprived and backward, the fact remains that the policy discriminates between followers

of different religions in a secular country by favouring a few. The moot point is, why do we need to identify the poor or needy in the name of religion? Are the poor confined to certain religious denominations? Or are the poor to be found in every segment and area of the country cutting across all castes, creeds, religions? If the socially, economically and educationally backward are found in villages and cities, amongst followers of all religions, in all castes and classes of people, then is it not necessary to identify them on common criterion applicable to all and not give backwardness the colour of religion and caste?

Hence, there is a the need to deal with the backward or backwardness comprehensively today and to consider issues and approaches followed so far, to deal with backwardness. It is also important to examine the norms applied to identify them and assess their appropriateness and suitability, for applying to all households across religions/castes in conformity with the objectives enshrined in the Constitution. I have chosen to speak on 'backwards' or 'backwardness' as it is intrinsically related to all policies and programmes meant for the deprived and discriminated. While discussing the dimensions of policies for minority appeasement, the reference is to the interventions being made for religious minority communities for the uplift of the socially and economically backward amongst them. The objection or concern is not to the interventions for ameliorating the backward status of those entitled amongst minorities, but the manner in which backwardness is being given the colour of religion especially when the facilities and services are available to them in equal measure from all programmes of the government.

Backwardness, its features and dimensions, therefore, need a closer and comprehensive examination. The fact that ours is a multi-racial, multi-religious and multi-lingual country with wide variations and inequalities, accentuated by regional and traditional disparities, was recognized by the framers of our Constitution. The policies of the Government of India and the state governments have been guided by the Constitutional provisions and goals it has set for the country. The ultimate objective, as laid down by the Constitution, is of a country secular in nature, based on the principles of equality, social justice and equity for all its citizens without discrimination on the basis of caste, creed, sex or religion. In conformity with the Constitutional directives, a two pronged strategy has been evolved for enhancing the status of the socially and economically backward, amongst different classes including the minorities. They are eligible for benefits from all policies and programmes of the government as they are non discriminatory in nature. Additionally, special provisions have been made for Scheduled Castes, Scheduled Tribes, Backward Classes, weaker sections and minorities to ensure greater thrust for accelerated development to bring them at par with the general categories. Needless to say, these programmes and interventions have enabled positive discrimination in favour of the backwards for their educational, social and economic development.

In order to appreciate the steps taken by the government to ameliorate the backward status of selected categories, it is essential to understand the logic and reasons behind the criteria adopted for their identification. Special provisions were made in the Constitution for distinct groups such as the Scheduled Castes,

Scheduled Tribes, Socially and educationally backward classes and weaker sections. The different approaches adopted for identifying them need to be noted.

The Scheduled Caste List was adopted as a special group by the Constitution of India in 1950 on the basis of Government of India Act, 1935 which had notified the special group titled 'Depressed Classes' in the 1931 Census as 'Scheduled Castes'. The criteria adopted for specifying the SCs was based on the obnoxious practice of untouchability. The test applied was the social, educational and economic backwardness arising out of the historical custom of untouchability.

The criteria applied for identifying the Scheduled Tribes as a separate category was the geographical isolation of the tribals which was responsible for their backwardness. Tribals include minorities as the criterion for identifying the STs are religion and caste neutral.

In view of the Constitution recognizing other socially and economically backward classes who may require special attention under Articles 15, 16(4), and 46, the Government of India appointed two Backward Classes Commissions–Kaka Kalelkar Commission in 1953 and Mandal Commission in 1979. GOI did not accept the recommendations of the Kaka Kalelkar Commission which recommended economic criteria as against that of caste. In 1961, GOI advised States to use their own discretion to choose criteria for defining backwardness. The Report of the Mandal Commissions given in 1980 was accepted after a gap of over a decade. It identified backward classes on the basis of social, educational and economic criteria. It should be noted that except for the Scheduled Caste List which is religion based for historical reasons, the list of Scheduled Tribes and Backward Classes are religion and caste neutral and hence include classes belonging to religious minorities. The criterion for identifying the STs and BCs are not determined by caste or religion.

The Government of India had constituted the National Commission for Religious and Linguistic Minorities for suggesting criteria for identifying the socially and economically backward amongst the religious and linguistic minorities in 2005. In this context, the Commission examined the existing status of different categories of backwards and the Constitutional and other provisions for them. The National Commission for Religious and Linguistic Minorities, in its report also examined the effectiveness of the criteria and the limitations and shortfalls in the procedures. The Commission further examined the impact of developmental initiatives on different categories and noted their status.

It is apparent from the foregoing that a differential approach was adopted to identify the socially and economically backward. While caste and religion based traditional deprivation and discrimination on the basis of the practice of untouchability determined the special status of SCs, tribals were given special status on account of physical and geographical isolation. Socially and educationally backward classes were enlisted for special dispensation at the Central and State level. The concept of a creamy layer was introduced, as it was accepted that no class was socially and educationally backward and poor as a whole and therefore those in the creamy layer would not be eligible for benefits from special policies and programmes. Guidelines for assessing socio-economic and educational status for determining households below and above the creamy layer have been issued by the National Commission for Backward Classes.

In spite of the improvements as a result of developmental initiatives, the question which agitates a growing number in the country is why the demand and need for identifying backwards even after 60 years of independence? Who are the backwards and how do we determine them, are still open questions for the government. Perhaps it is due to the segregated and sectarian approach adopted towards backwardness. The issues to focus on in this regard are:

- The number of SCs, STs and OBCs has increased manifold. The first notification of 1950 included 607 SC communities which were raised to 1109 by 2002. While 502 castes have been additionally added to the initial list, only 33 castes have been excluded over the years. The number of STs notified in 1950 was 240; it has increased to 628. There have been only 15 exclusions. The Backward Classes list, which included 1,238 classes comprising of classes common to Mandal Commission and States, now has 2,159 communities. The issue is–are more and more of us are becoming 'backward'?
- The government's policies and provisions have developed a stake in remaining/claiming backward status to take advantage of concessions, reservations, and positive discriminations. It is perhaps because there is no regular system to review and revise the lists of backwards or of SCs/STs on an ongoing basis, at regular intervals, to ensure that those who have benefited from the special policies and programmes and are no longer poor are excluded from the lists so that they do not continue

to access advantages, for generations, at the cost of the more deserving. The absence of a system to monitor social and economic progress has further resulted in the belief that once a backward, always a backward, for the purposes of subsidies, special benefits etc!

- The criteria for identifying the backwards is faulty and does not deter or exclude those who have gained from the policies and programmes and are no longer socio-economically poor, from continuing to obtain benefits. The burgeoning middle classes in each category have developed vested interests and organize themselves as pressure groups to remain backward as the policy of segregated approach encourages each group and category to claim backward status. There is no rational system for correctly assessing the income of those not within the tax fold. This leaves room for inaccurate reporting and the number of backward and poor growing continuously despite the investments in development over the last 60 years.
- While modifications in SC and ST list can be done by Parliament alone, OBCs list can be changed as per recommendations of the Backward Classes Commission and other categories can be added by Government No assessment of population to be added is made while recommending, nor surveys conducted to assess socio-economic status. Additions are made, by and large on account of political and other compulsions. Hence the demand by groups on grounds beyond constitutional provisions.
- The increasing trend by groups and classes perceived to be economically and socially better off, using pressure tactics for

gaining entry as OBCs, if not in any category, and as SC or ST if enjoying status of OBC, is an issue. For example in recent years the inclusion of Jats as Backward Class, the demand by Gujjars for inclusion, demand by Muslims and Christians for status of SCs, by Jats in Haryana for inclusion are a clear indication that the reasons for demand are not backwardness, but political and other gains.

- Since backwardness is not a characteristic of a caste, class or religion in entirety and each comprises of the rich, middle income and poor households, including or excluding any caste, class or followers of a religion as 'backward' as a whole, would either unjustly deprive the poor or give benefits to the ineligible within that group. The issue at stake is the suitability of the existing system based on discriminatory norms to help all backwards.
- We have two parallel systems for identifying the poor backward. The segregated approach as mentioned above and a comprehensive universally applicable one to all categories of people for identifying the families/households Below Poverty Line. The latter includes households included after a survey, to assess their social, economic and educational status. The issue is, why the need for multiplicity of lists of backwards. It complicates the issue and deprives the poorest from getting benefits. After 60 years of concerted action for development, the need is to do away with the SC, ST and OBC lists in favour of a uniform single list rather than add castes or religious groups.

The number of backward classes has increased, despite investments in developmental activities and special provisions and policy initiatives of positive discrimination in favour of SCs, STs,

OBCs and minorities over the last several decades. More classes or castes or tribes becoming 'backward', should ordinarily raise doubts about the efficacy of strategies, policies and programmes evolved and implemented, for raising the socio-economic status of the backward and weaker communities. Despite tardy implementation of policies and programmes, the status of each category has improved. The Census data stands testimony to the progression.

This only indicates that considerations other than backwardness—vested interests, political considerations, pressure tactics by vested groups etc—are responsible for the swelling numbers of SCs, STs and OBCs. A stake appears to have developed in remaining 'backward' which is neither conducive to equity and social justice nor to the integrity of the nation.

The rationale of the policies is apparent. The special dispensation to certain categories on account of traditional discrimination or deprivation was to be given for a limited time. Unfortunately, over the last few decades instead of class, caste or religious differences narrowing, the segregated and discriminatory approach of the State has accentuated the differences and increased the demand for special treatment by classes and religious groups including those who were never recognized as backward. Though ours is a multi-religious, multi-racial society with wide variations on regional basis, no community, caste or religious group can be called rich or poor exclusively. It is households which can be identified as backward. The factors that determine backwardness are economic, social and educational and not religion or caste. Indices such as income, educational standard, work participation, mortality rates, life expectancy, health and nutritional status etc are taken to determine developmental status.

Education is an important determinant of social and economic development. The educational and literacy levels amongst various categories including the minority communities vary considerably from one community to the other and one area to another. Christians, Jains and Parsis have higher educational status than Muslims and Buddhists. However, their levels are higher than SCs and STs. Disaggregated Census data presents a picture of unevenness in the educational status of Muslims and Buddhists cutting across states. In states like Bihar, Madhya Pradesh, Rajasthan, Uttar Pradesh and other under-developed and backward States, the poor and the socially and economically backward of each community including the Muslims, present a dismal picture as all of them are equal victims and suffer equally from disabilities and depravations. In developed states, the status of minorities is higher and is comparable with others in that State. For example, the literacy levels of Muslims are high in Kerala. Demanding or identifying socially and economically backward on the basis of caste, class or religion is therefore, neither just nor equitable.

Identifying castes, classes as backward was perhaps based on the belief that the entire caste comprised of backwards. Our Constitution provided relief to categories which had faced discrimination or depravation for centuries on account of either the low status accorded or geographical isolation. For the reasons given, there was justification for specially categorizing them and giving them special consideration. However, these were meant to be short term interventions and it was expected that the caste distinctions will narrow down with their accelerated growth. It was not expected that the number of categories and the grounds for expanding coverage would perpetually increase. There are some fallacies and myths about status which are not borne out by facts and data. NCAER's annual household survey of income shows that at an all India level in 2004-05 upper caste households earned an average of Rs 86,690 per annum, OBCs Rs 59,741, SCs Rs 45,889, and STs Rs 40,753. However, the averages miss out the important differences which an analysis of the NCAER's data clearly brings out. It establishes that incomes across caste groups differ widely across various states, meaning thereby, that overall development of the state is more important than the caste of an individual when it comes to determining income levels. ST households in Karnataka earn more than Upper caste households in Bihar and SC households earn more than the same caste households in UP. Caste, class or religion is thus not an appropriate or judicious indicator of backwardness for all in a category.

The analysis also establishes that differences in income do not automatically imply discrimination. Apart from the state of development, education, type of industry/service an individual is employed in and the location–rural or urban, small town or metro–also impacts the income levels. These factors determine the income levels of other categories including minorities as well. In the case of Muslims, another factor affecting their backwardness is that they have the highest proportion of self-employed households in non-agricultural occupations. The solution is not a segregated caste or religion based approach to 'backwardness, but a uniform strategy for identifying the poor households and adopting a differential approach for development which is vocation and occupation based. The National Commissions and Finance Corporations fulfil special requirements.

There is an urgent need to rise above segregated demands and pressures to adopt a comprehensive and universally applicable criterion for the entire country cutting across religions, castes, creeds etc. The special provisions for specific categories under the Constitution were meant to be time bound. After 60 years, if the demand for inclusion in categories of backwards or for being given the benefits available to SCs/STs is growing, it is a cause for serious concern. More and more communities are demanding backward status because they see great advantages in being recognized as backward. The policy of including classes and communities as backward, without any scientific system of assessing status or numbers, with no fear of exclusion since the system doesn't provide for it, is a very attractive proposition especially for those who have gained from the programmes. There is adequate evidence to show that the advantages from various programmes are going to the haves at the cost of the really deserving have-nots.

Unless the system ensures that the upwardly mobile are excluded on an ongoing basis, the benefits will continue to flow to the more advanced in each category in perpetuity. Caste and religion when adopted as determinants of 'backwardness', introduce a dimension into the process of identification which is inherently discriminatory and nurtures a feeling of depravation in the categories excluded. It also gives credence to the concept of appeasement and in this case 'minority appeasement' which a secular nation as ours should not follow. A rational approach is necessary to ensure that no segment feels discriminated or deprived.

Backwardness has neither a caste nor a religion. Religion and Caste are undoubtedly a part of our present reality. But in consonance with the aims and objectives of the Constitution it is not for the State to differentiate between its citizens on the basis of caste or religion. As Andre Beteille, a well known social scientist, says the State should not "give recognition to caste or religion for official purposes without special or valid reasons." It is the States interventions on the basis of religion to the minorities–the largest beneficiaries being the Muslims–that seems to be accentuating differences and increasing tensions and contravening the objectives of our Constitution of a non-discriminatory State.

The ostensible reason for special dispensation to minorities is said to be their socio-economically backward status vis-à-vis other categories. The data on literacy, income, life expectancy, IMR etc of minorities compared to SCs, STs establishes that their status varies from state to state as it is determined by the general state of development prevailing in the area. Their status is generally higher than that of SCs and STs and in most states compares with that of other categories, including Hindus. However, even if they are poorer, the common criterion will enlist all eligible, making separate enumeration redundant.

As I mentioned earlier backwardness is not limited to a single religion or caste or class. The Census data on people below poverty line and on developmental indices of various categories—Hindus, minorities, Scheduled castes, Scheduled Tribes, and OBCs establishes beyond doubt that there are socially, economically and educationally backward people in substantial numbers in all categories, including the Hindus. BPL data is collected for a household as a unit and is the most comprehensive enumeration on universally applicable norms. As per the NSSO data of 2004-05 the population of families Below Poverty Line (BPL) was 30.8 per cent, of SCs 38.7 per cent, STs 48.4 per cent, OBCs 33.1 per cent and General category 18.2 per cent. The minorities are included in all lists except that of SCs. As per the 2001 Census, with reference to the sex-ratio in general and in the age group of 0-6, all minority communities except Sikhs have a higher ratio than average. Hindus in both cases have a lower ratio than Muslims. Similar is the case with regard to other indices. The differences vary, but in most cases the status of minorities is higher than that of SCs and STs.

In the 60 years or more of independence, we have had Five-Year Plans and economic liberalization; agrarian reforms and industrial development; adult franchise and Panchayati Raj; and host of legal, constitutional and other changes. A plethora of policies and programmes have been evolved and implemented to reach out to the deprived and poor, of all categories, through both non-discriminatory and discriminatory special programmes. Both, the impact of these on households needs and the adverse impact of the State interventions need to be recognized and assessed. It is well recognized that in the last two to three decades, we have introduced elements into State policies which have increased the numbers of 'backwards' in the country manifold. The policy has given rise to increasing demands for inclusion in the lists of SCs, STs, OBCs and by religious groups despite the fact that they form a part of all categories except SCs. In the last few decades, the number of SCs, STs and OBCs has increased substantially, with negligible exclusions. We also know that the system prescribed for inclusion on the basis of demands is not scientific or rational. Yet there is little or no effort to set right the system and adopt strategies, which will unite people and help to identify and review eligible backwards, intermittently, to ensure that benefits flow to the deserving only.

Religion, caste and class-based discriminatory policies have no doubt accentuated differences. They also appear to have introduced an element of organized action amongst backward categories, to seek recognition through inclusion, to take advantage of government/official schemes and programmes on a continuing basis. These vested interests are aware that the system has no scientific method for assessing eligibility and enforcing exclusion thereafter. In fact, this is the major cause, for benefits from various programmes not reaching the poorest, as the poor and needy lack the wherewithal to access institutions and organizations, which are meant to deliver the services to them. Agitations by Jats and Gujjars for pressurising the government for inclusion and of Christians and Muslims for inclusion as SCs are some of the examples of the race for inclusion, irrespective of their status.

The rise in atrocities committed on the basis of caste and community is another indicator of the adverse impact of policies that discriminate on irrational grounds and are divisive. The rising trend of intolerance—the latest being on a teacher in Kerala and the authorities succumbing to the pressure tactics of a community are also dimensions of the policies being adopted and expanded, on grounds, which are discriminatory in nature.

From a peaceful society that prided itself as a multi-religious, multicultural nation, the last few decades have witnessed growing trend in dissensions and intolerance amongst different castes and religious groups where none existed. These are all wake-up calls not only for those who govern, but for the society as a whole and call for corrective measures urgently.

We have overlapping systems which allow inclusion in more than one list today. There is a great deal of overlap in the OBCs, SCs, STs, minorities and BPL lists. The present system, therefore, allows duplication and facilitates access to benefits from more than one list, for want of proper checks, to a selected few at the cost of the poor backwards who continue to be deprived of opportunities for their development.

Besides, the criteria adopted for identifying the backwards under different categories also differs. While both the OBCs and BPL families are identified on the basis of socio-economic criterion, the yardstick applied in both varies. Except for BPL lists which are revised on the basis of socio-economic survey of households every five years, the remaining categories have no procedure laid down for regular review on objective and universally applicable principles. The result is, that the system leaves room for biases, vested interests, subjective assessments and political and other considerations to play a part. We see the impact in the increasing demand for inclusion and a growing sense of dissatisfaction in different groups.

It is, therefore, necessary to identify the poor and backward households across the country, by adopting religion and caste neutral criterion which is universally applicable, based on factors that determine the social, economic and educational status of each.

It is not that the government has not set up Commissions for the exclusive task of suggesting criteria for identifying backward groups. In recent years, the GOI had set up the National Commission for Religious and Linguistic Minorities for suggesting criteria for identifying socio-economically backward amongst the minorities. It also set up an Economically Backward Classes Commission to suggest criterion for identifying the poor and backward amongst the general categories. It is obvious that the Government is aware that no religion, caste, or class, including the general categories, is exclusively rich or poor, developed or backward. All categories are an amalgam of people with different social and economic status. Hence, no class should be declared as a backward class as a whole nor should it be eligible for benefits from government schemes formulated to help the socio-economically deprived. It was this knowledge which prompted the government to introduce the concept of creamy layer for eliminating the economically better-off from accessing subsidies and other special dispensations. Incomes in rural areas and of non-income tax payers are difficult to assess in our country, which leaves great scope for inclusion and continuation in perpetuity of the non-eligible. Rather than add a whole class as backward and then exclude the better off, the better option is to declare only the backward and poor households as backward. It would facilitate uniformity in action and prevent subjective elements and pressure tactics from influencing inclusions.

The compulsions for continuing a segregated approach to backwards which is accentuating differences, encouraging the organized sections of the groups to use pressure tactics and even hold governments to ransom for grant of illegal demands are difficult to understand. As an alternate system, for identifying the socially and economically poor which is more scientific and rational, already exists and is under implementation, i.e., the BPL list, it stands to reason that it should be adopted without wasting any more time. The existing system where caste, class or religions are adopted as criterion is inappropriate and unsuitable for identifying the socially and economically deprived. They are neither based on scientific principles nor surveys and have no provision for regular review to exclude those who have progressed. It is, therefore, necessary in the interest of the country to discontinue a system that applies different yardsticks to identify the poor belonging to different religions, castes or classes, which are neither equitable nor just and leave room for extraneous, discriminatory and subjective assessments, not in consonance with our constitutional objectives and an integrated cohesive society. There is an urgent need to stem the tide, which the existing system has let loose on the helpless poor, who stand to lose either way under the present system.

As mentioned above, households below poverty line are enlisted after a survey conducted every five years on the basis of 13 indices which determine the socio-economic status of the households. A uniform pattern and criteria for identifying backwards based on economic and educational parameters irrespective of caste and religion as is applicable for BPL list should be adopted, to replace the existing lists of SCs, STs, OBCs and BPL families. It will be a list based on secular criteria and will therefore further the principles of equality, equity, justice and non-discrimination enshrined in our Constitution. The following steps are suggested:

- Household should be adopted as the unit for determining the educational and economic backwardness.
- An evaluation study be undertaken to assess the adequacy and suitability of existing criteria adopted for identifying the BPL households. Though it is all inclusive and should cover SCs, STs, OBCs, and minorities, gaps and shortfalls in coverage and flow of benefits should be examined and modifications made. The coverage of all backwards of all categories in the BPL list will automatically remove the overlap, different categories including minorities' have in the existing list.
- A time-bound schedule for having one list of the socially, economically and educationally backward cutting across caste, religion or other discriminations should be evolved and accepted.
- A detailed socio-economic household survey should be conducted for identifying the backwards in rural and urban areas on the basis of norms evolved for each, taking into account the nature of the problem and the differences between the rural and urban populations. A universal survey will automatically include all communities leaving no reason for separate demands.
- The list so prepared should be revised every five years on the basis of a universal survey. Village level and city level local bodies should be involved in the processes both for inclusion and exclusion and a system for redress of complaints set up. Participation of local bodies will encourage accountability and result in better implementation.

These are just a few suggestions. Any change and specially the withdrawal or reduction in benefits and facilities to groups is bound to be opposed by the vested groups. But if we have to curb the divisive trends gaining further ground, in the interest of the large numbers of poor and backward, we have no choice but to ensure that the government adopts systems and programmes that are based on universally applicable norms on an equal basis for the backward and poor of all classes and communities. We need to generate awareness regarding the ill effects of policies which are dividing the society and/or organizing it on the lines of caste, class or religion amongst all segments cutting across regions so that a demand for one yardstick for all irrespective of caste or creed in the country is realized. There is enough evidence to suggest that a large segment of the poor and backward in the country remain unreached by the policies and programmes meant for them. The identification of backwards across castes, classes and religions on the lines of BPL households will facilitate focus on the development of the eligible and deserving only. The adoption of one list of backwards will leave no room for allegations of 'appeasement' and curb the growing tensions leading to atrocities between caste and religious groups. With the Sarva Shiksha Abhiyan to ensure education to every child in the country and the emphasis on vocational training and schemes like NREGA etc to counter poverty through employment, the time is opportune for replacing divisive strategies by uniformly applicable interventions.

Dimensions of Minority Appeasement

— Bal Apte

Definition of Minority

The word 'minority' means many things to many people. It has various meanings and in the Indian context it means different things to different people. Let us look at some accepted definitions used worldwide and the Indian usage. The United Nations, for its purposes, takes into account the following definition:

> Minorities are "A group of people numerically inferior to the rest of the population of a state, in a non-dominant position, whose members–being nationals of the state–possess ethnic, religious or linguistic characteristics differing from those of the rest of the population, and show, if only implicitly, a sense of solidarity, directed towards preserving their culture, tradition, religion or language."
>
> — Special Rapporteur Francesco Capotorti, for the Sub-Commission on Prevention of Discrimination and Protection of Minorities of the UN.

After a review of all earlier attempts at an accurate definition, A S Akermark[1] defines minority as,

> "A non-dominant, institutionalised group sharing a distinct cultural identity that it wishes to preserve."

How the ruling British saw 'minorities' and the self-perception of the Muslim leadership is evident in the address presented to Viceroy Lord Minto by a 'Deputation of Muslim Community of India' on 1 October 1906. The deputation said:

> "We...urge that the position accorded to the Mohammedan community in any kind of representation...should be commensurate, not merely with their numerical strength, but also with their political importance...and to give due consideration to the position which they occupied in India a little more than hundred years ago...."

Lord Minto replied:

> "...(The) Mohammedan community may rest assured that their political rights and interests as a community will be safeguarded."

Concept of 'minority' in India

The concept went through two phases:

(a) Under the British Rule

(b) Developments in international relations, after the Great Wars and dissolution of empires (that is after 1945)

Under the British Rule

This is how the idea of the 'minority' evolved during the years that a free Indian constitution was debated in the pre-Independence years–that is during the Indian Constitutional Progression, right through the Constituent Assembly days. In–

1. 1909 the Morley-Minto Reforms took place. Separate electoral rights to Muslims and Europeans (as minorities) were considered
2. 1910 Census: (a) Hindus, (b) Tribes, (c) Dalits were separately enumerated
3. 1916 Lucknow: the Congress-League Scheme was formulated Substantial political representation was accorded in Councils to 'minorities': only Muslims are mentioned
4. 1932 Communal Award, Poona Pact, Government of India Act 1919 Government of India Act 1935 all came into effect.

Representation to minorities in governance was given to the following communities:

a. Anglo-Indians
b. Europeans
c. Indian Christians
d. Parsees
e. Sikhs
f. Scheduled Castes (Depressed Classes)

5. Then came the framing of the Constitution by the Constituent Assembly (This process was boycotted by the Muslim League). The recommendations by the Constituent Assembly were through an:

(i) Advisory Committee Report, 8 August 1947 which suggested joint electorates with reservation to minorities:

Group A: Anglo-Indians, Parsees and Plains-tribes-men in Assam

Group B: Indian Christians and Sikhs

Group C: Muslims and Scheduled Castes

(ii) After Partition (August 1947)

The Advisory Committee appointed a special sub-committee and placed its report before the Constituent Assembly (with the concurrence of the members of the minority communities on the committee) in 11 May 1949. This report said: 'The system of reservation for minorities other than Scheduled Castes in Legislatures be abolished.'

'In the long run, it would be in the interest of all to forget that there is anything like majority or minority in this country and that in India there is only one community', Sardar Patel said in the Constituent Assembly on 25 May 1949.

Meanwhile, the United Nations was devising its own definition of minorities in a post-World War world. The word 'minority' meant something in the 1920s but acquired more specific meaning after 1940. Internationally, the word went through three phases of evolution after the First World War

International Developments

'Minority' after World War I and dissolution of empires:

1. Ottoman
2. Czar
3. Austro-Hungarian and Prussian.

The League of Nations was created after the end of World War I. The Versailles Peace Treaty was signed and the Paris Peace Conference was convened in January 1919. The Covenant of the League of Nations was adopted on 28 April 1919.

In a way the winners, the US, the UK and some others took

control of the world and with a declared objective of lasting peace and international cooperation, went about establishing states with international obligations.

As described, in this upheaval of history, territories were re-distributed and new borders were drawn. New territories were incorporated in already existing states, and new states were created and recognized.

All this was done by treaties with all such states.

All this redrawing of boundaries resulted in putting many communities in countries to which they did not volunteer to go. It became the duty of the system that did this, to protect their rights; hence the concept of "Minority Protection."

Treaties were signed with Poland, Serbs, Croats, Slovenes, Czechoslovakia, Romania, Greece, Austria, Bulgaria, Hungary and Turkey.

New states were declared—Albania, Lithuania, Latvia, Estonia and Iraq being prominent examples.

Thus, the concept of minority protection was part of treaties under the League of Nations. These ethnic, religious or linguistics minorities were citizens of the respective states because of their inclusion in the new boundaries of these states.

At the international level, Human Rights became the subject of further discourse and the rights of minorities were part of that under the subsequent UN system.

The issue was of day-to-day importance in the European situation and hence the subject matter of several European Documents, which we may not go into.

It is at the end of the World War II that the United Nations came into being. The definition of minority took new shape under the UN in two distinct stages.

Under the UN System

1. The International Covenant on Civil and Political Rights (1966) Art. 27 says: In those states in which ethnic, religious or linguistic minorities exist, persons belonging to such minorities shall not be denied the right, in community with the other members of their group, to enjoy their own culture, to profess and practice their own religion, or to use their own language.
2. The Declaration on the Rights of Persons belonging to national or ethnic, religious and linguistic minorities (1992) says: The preamble of this Declaration views them (minorities) 'as an integral part of the development of society as a whole and within a democratic framework based on the Rule of Law'.

Minority under the Indian Constitution

In the chapter on Fundamental Rights in the Indian Constitution, the protection of interests of minorities is enumerated under the sub-heading 'Cultural and Educational Rights' in two Articles, Articles 29 and 30.

The scope of these articles was enlarged by judicial pronouncements which can be justly criticized. Articles 25 to 28 under the sub-heading 'Right to freedom of Religion' are, sometimes, erroneously treated as part of minority protection. In the same way, secularism is erroneously equated with the rights of minorities.

It is interesting to note, without comment, the progress of

the T M A Pai Foundation's writ petition in the Supreme Court. While examining the rights of the minority institutions to admit students without following the criterion of common entrance test, the Bench raised a question as to what is a 'minority'. The question was referred to a larger bench. Ultimately, the case went to a larger bench of eleven judges. In the process, the original question 'what is a minority' was lost. The 11-judge bench did not answer the additional five questions, one of them being: what is 'religion'?

As a matter of academic interest, it may be mentioned that the ratio of this 11-judge bench decision was explained by a '5-judge bench' and that was overruled by a ruling of a '7-judge bench'!

The notable points regarding Muslims as a minority

They do not fall under the internationally accepted definition.

They were never in a non-dominant position in this country.

They did not want protection.

They demanded rights as former rulers.

The notable points regarding Christians as a minority

They belonged to the ruling class.

They extracted the right to propagate religion as a fundamental right, which is not available under any Constitution of the world.

History of Appeasement

1. During the British Rule: The Congress was over-anxious to get Muslim participation in the freedom movement, hence the concessions and appeasement policy which began with the following steps:

- Lucknow Pact
- Khilafat Movement
- Killer of Swami Shraddhananda praised as Rashid 'Bhai' by Mahatma Gandhi
- The song Vande Mataram was abridged and later abandoned
- The saffron flag was not adopted
- In Constitution making separate electorate was accepted

2. After Independence
    - Concessions to Pakistan (transfer of assets/revenue)
    - The Nehru-Liaquat Pact
    - The Rann of Kutch (concession)
    - Kashmir (division)

After India became a Republic came the vote-bank politics. The policies adopted post 1950s included:

- Soft on terrorists and Bangladeshi infiltrators
- Denial of legitimate Hindu rights

The United Progressive Alliance's appeasements included:

- Sachar Committee
- Ranganath Mishra Commission
- PM's 15-point programme
- Minority Institutions Legislation
- Andhra: Communal Reservation
- Aligarh: Communal Reservation
- Targeting Gujarat
- Targeting the Ram Sethu
- Official Discrimination against the Amarnath Yatra
- Kandhamal: Murder of Swami Laxmananand

- Aligarh campuses in Muslim-majority districts from West Bengal to Kerala
- No reservations in minority educational institutions.

Minority Protection under Articles 29 & 30 of the Constitution

1. For citizens of India
2. For linguistic and religious minorities; there is no ethnic minority
3. State-specific status of both
4. Not above the law of the land
5. No reverse discrimination

(Law as laid down in the case of TMA Pai Foundation v/s State of Karnataka WP (Civil) No. 31711993 decided on 31-10-2002) (11-judge bench orders)

Dimensions of Minority Appeasement

1. Further divisiveness, separation, ghettoisation.
2. The purpose of minority protection is to develop a homogeneous society. The appeasement policy achieves a converse purpose of keeping them separate and fighting. It creates an intolerant minority.
3. It is useful to ponder over the following observations of Ramesh Chandra in 'Ethnic Minorities and Identity Politics': The issue of segregating national minority study modules into an elective designed to extend specific knowledge to a self-selected audience raises the issue of whether the purpose of these norms is simply to ensure access by national minorities to an education that includes their own culture or to ensure

the development of a society based on a tolerant and diverse citizenry. An Organization for Economic Cooperation and Development (OECD) report published in September 2001 suggests that 'education systems should not just be 'fair' to minorities–they should promote a spirit of equality and tolerance among ethnic and cultural groups.' In a report on minority rights in education in Estonia, Latvia, Romania and Macedonia, it is similarly concluded that:

"Learning does not encourage living together" and that there is a danger of a strictly mono-lingual/mono-religious/mono-cultural or even mono-racial approach, leading to ghettoisation of minorities. The results of exclusive Madrassa-education are there for all to see.

4. A deliberate attempt to alienate the Muslim minority from the mainstream has a direct impact in the form of threat of jihadi terror to the civilizations of the world. Ghettoisation, alienation and propagandist education breeds a sense of injury and anger, which finds an outlet that is provided with cool precision. Today, this comes in the form of what can be called the "cocktail of Koran with Kalashnikov."

References

1. Akermark, *Justification of Minority Protection in International Law*, Kluiver Law International, The Hague
2. Kymlicka, *Politics in the Vernacular*, Oxford University Press, USA (2001)

3. Ed Kashyap, *The Framing of India's Constitution Vol. 1 to 6,* Universal
4. *Government of India Acts*, Constitution of India
5. Ghandhi, *Blackstone's International Human Rights Documents,* OUP Oxford (2006)
6. Khanna, *Making of India's Constitution*, Eastern Book Company
7. Ed Pramod Shah, *Thought on Religious Politics in India Vol.1 to 3*, Society for National Awareness, Kolkata
8. Constituent Assembly debates

Kerala in the land of Adi Sankara?

— C I Issac

On the eve of our national freedom, the leadership of the minority [Semitic] religious sects of this land firmly supported the British Raj for various reasons. Their negative approach is no doubt the greatest betrayal in the five thousand years of our well-accredited history. The Muslims along with their leadership stood for Dar-ul-Islam and the church, irrespective of its liturgical contradictions, prayed at its altars for the perpetual continuance of the British Empire in India. It is the greatest paradox that Fr Jerome De Souza, the Principal of Loyola College, Madras, a native of Mangalore, represented the Christian community of India in the Constitution Drafting Committee of India. This is notwithstanding the fact that several educated Christians of the day who joined in the national movement and were subjected to the wrath of the church, including excommunication, were ignored when the Constitution Drafting Committee was constituted. Doubtless this happened because of grave errors on the part of those on the political side.

Nonetheless, this points out in detail the process of evolution of the state policy of minority appeasement. Subsequently, the traitorous church, which before independence had sympathized with the British Crown, began to monopolize the fruits of the newly-obtained freedom in the name of minority. The 'ruling dynasty' of India for long has been dancing to the vested interests of minority priesthoods. The earliest of this kind was the incorporation of minority rights (Article 29 & 30) in the constitution, with scant regard to the tradition of this land[1], an act that really intensified the alienation of religious minorities from the national mainstream. Much before the infamous 42nd amendment of the Constitution in 1976 (Preamble), the concept of socialism and secularism had been well ingrained in Hindu society for millions of years. Correspondingly, the incorporation of Article 370 remains a stumbling block in the way of integration and is the worst specimen of the Nehruvian perfidy of minority appeasement.

The history of minority religious appeasement in Kerala goes back to the days of vote-bank building of the Communist movement. The Communists built up their vote-banks in the backward Hindu *jatis* of Kerala by alienating them from the age-old reciprocal social structure of the Hindu society by breaking its weakest links, through the exaggeration of untoward practices that existed before the states' Renaissance stewarded by Shree Narayana Guru and Chattambi Swamikal. This ultimately resulted in the birth of a divided and highly polarized Hindu society. This success of the Communist strategy was countered by the Congress through creating vote-banks amongst the religious minorities through a policy of appeasement. Above all, the Congress Party was well aware of the potential of the church. The minorities, particularly the Catholics, have been using their educational institutions as a weapon against the ruling governments of Kerala since the forties of the last century. Whenever they were in confrontation with the ruling governments they used to shutdown their education institutions as a retaliatory measure, creating social problems. The church has a formidable track record in inflaming communal feelings amongst its laity through reading pastoral letters in the midst of holy mass. During 1958, the "liberation movement" against the first elected communist ministry and in 1971 to defuse governmental attempt to effect social control over colleges, they used the same weapon effectively against democratic governments. Subsequently, the CPI (M) also adopted the Congress policy of minority appeasement in a more professional and competitive manner by sacrificing the interests of the Hindu community in general and particularly of their vote-bank *jatis*. Thus it ushered in the new political equation of coalition rule.

The major beneficiaries of the Kerala model of coalition politics are the minorities of the Abrahamic religions. The pastoral function of their religious hierarchy enhanced the bargaining capacity of the minorities in the pragmatic politics of Kerala. Above all, these minorities still retain their own political parties. When a coalition ministry is formed, the minority representation in the cabinet will be much higher than the Hindus because the national parties are forced to accommodate minorities in order to maintain a "secular" fig-leaf, whereas the constituent partner of the coalition, i.e., the minority-sponsored religious parties, secure cabinet berths exclusively for their community. In effect, the equilibrium of the cabinet always favours the minorities in two ways; viz, prominent portfolios as well as a majority of ministries go to religious minorities.

Take a glaring instance: in the 54 years since the formation of the state of Kerala, who has controlled the portfolio of education? For 25 years, it was under the control of the Muslim League and for another ten years and three months, in the hands of Catholic-controlled Kerala Congress. National and secular parties could acquire the portfolio only for 18 years and in this duration only four years and three months with a minister with a Hindu name. If this isn't really shocking information to a nationalist, pray, what is? In fact, without any intermission, granting of pension to *mullas* and peons (*mukris*) of the Madrassa to the indiscriminate establishment of Arabic colleges–all were carried out at the expense of the state exchequer. Several posts of Arabic high school teachers were created in the aided and government schools and illiterate Muslims were appointed as "teachers" on the basis of a certificate issued by *mullas*. An exclusive Sanskrit university was established in the name of Adi Sankara at his birthplace, Kaladi. The worst irony is that the University is on the path of 'halal', slaughtering of the existing possibilities of Sanskrit, in the heady rush to promote Urdu and Arabic. Even in the matter of the State School Youth festival, the education department is intensively investigating how to Islamize and Christianize the content of the festival. All these are the backdrop of the ongoing vote-bank politics of Kerala.

Minority appeasement is a way of political life in Kerala. It was shepherded in at the dawn of our freedom. It is instructive to scrutinize the pages of history to see, to what extent Muslim bigots are agitated when a Muslim steps out of their faith. In 1946, one Muslim, Unnian Saheb, who after his return to Hinduism, acquired the name Ramasimhan, of Angadippuram of Calicut, along with his family returned to their *poorva dharma* (Hinduism). Agitated Muslim bigots led a bloodthirsty mob of Moplah (Muslims of coastal Kerala) and brutally exterminated Ramasimhan and his family, as an admonition to those wishing to return to their roots. But the hideous paradox is that all Abrahamic religions continue the act of conversion of Hindus unrestrictedly ever since they have set foot in this land. In the above case, all political parties, including the Marxist Party under its self-styled "revolutionary" leader EMS Namboodripad, attempted to misdirect the police investigation and save the culprits from the purview of law of the land.[2] Even the "secular" Jawaharlal Nehru interfered in the affair and instructed to hand over the sons of the deceased, under the protection of Ramakrishna Mission, to the Islamic fundamentalists. Thereafter, the political parties of Kerala continue the same minority appeasement policy without much difference.

As a result of the undeclared minority appeasement policy, the legislature, executive and judiciary of Kerala are in a dilemma since the days of the above-mentioned murder, whenever issues related to minority religious groups come before them for disposal. This pathetic situation of Kerala was once again demonstrated to the rest of India, when a Bangalore court issued an arrest warrant against a hard-core Muslim terrorist Abdul Nasser Madani. The governmental machineries of Kerala found themselves between the devil and the deep sea. This was but one more episode in the saga of minority religious appeasement of Kerala.

Those people's representatives, who had taken their oath of allegiance in complete contradiction of the constitutional directive, i.e., taking oath in the name of Allah and Infant Jesus instead of God, continue as ministers, MLAs and MPs. If a Hindu were to take an oath of allegiance in the name of his personal deity, it would be termed a "gross violation of the stipulations enshrined in the Constitution of India." The Kerala High Court's decision of 3 March 2003 in the case against Umesh Challiyil (MLA 2001-06) is an example to this embargo. All sorts of impertinence based on religion is the outcome of the coercive tactics employed by the state's organized minorities in the state, over years. It goes without saying that this sort of unbridled wantonness still enjoyed by the minorities of the state, is solely due to the unorganized condition of the Hindus.

The issue of the erection of the statue of Tunchathu Ezhuthachan, father of Malayalam language and literature, at his birthplace, Tirur (which falls under the jurisdiction of exclusive Muslim district Malappuram) has once again proved, fundamentalist Islam's inability to stomach an idol, as it is un-Islamic. Finally, the issue was settled with the erection of a symbolic representation of an ink pot and brush—the official emblem of Jamait-e-Islami—instead of his statue. It is true that Ezhuthachan in his poetical compositions used only the Stylus and the Palmyra leaf for writing on, and never used pen or ink. What is the mental inclination behind this fanaticism? No doubt, the ever-growing money and muscle power of the minorities in Kerala coupled with the shameful appeasement mentality of mainstream political parties.

From 1990 to date, Muslim fundamentalists have killed 20 Hindus, one Muslim and one Christian under the instruction of various Taliban "courts" [14 in number], which function all over Kerala. Recent disclosures point to the fact that they are running a parallel regime. As part of the policy of minority appeasement of the Left and United Front regimes, all the 21 cases of killing of Hindus were charged under normal criminal offences. The last victim was a Christian college professor, whose right hand was chopped off by a jihadist organization for setting a question paper "blasphemous to Islam." To appease the Christian leadership this case was properly investigated, which unearthed the density of the Islamic jihadist presence in Kerala; the major culprits were booked in a short duration. So far, both Fronts have patronized Islamic jihadists with competitive spirit. In short, an assault on a Hindu either by Communists or fundamentalist Muslims or Christians is no more a matter of concern, to either the political parties or the media. Minority appeasement prevails even in the approach to terrorism.

Catholic Churches declare unauthorized holidays in the state-aided educational institutions under their management; this has now become a customary affair. In the name of the mythical Saint Thomas's arrival in India, local church festivals, first Fridays, etc., are common holidays in the Catholic run-aided schools. The government of the state and related authorities remain mere onlookers before minority impertinence. For the festive days of every religious groups in Kerala other than Muslims, there is only one day as state-declared holiday. On the other hand, Muslims have had more than one day, as state-declared holidays for the last three decades. Is it justifiable? No doubt, all this largesse enjoyed by the minorities is improper and only confirm their organized bargaining power.

The States Women's Commission's proposal to the government for curbing the mysterious death of nuns in the Catholic convents of Kerala still remains a cry in the wilderness. Their effort to restrict the minimum age for entry into nun-hood at 18 was a creative proposal and a panacea for the ever-increasing baffling deaths in the convents. Neither the opposition nor the ruling party has shown any courage to debate the proposal in the Legislative Assembly or in any party forums. The ruling and opposition parties, as the part of their undeclared policy of minority appeasement, are in competition to deny social justice to the victims of the convent tragedies.

Hindus in Kerala are dangerously divided. Moreover, they are a highly politicized section of the state. Any attempt by the prime movers of the society to unite them will be aborted by political interference and through the stratagem of the minorities. Of such moves, one was the appointment of Narendran Commission. The main focus of the Commission was whether the socially and economically backward *jatis* of Kerala have appropriate representation in government services in Kerala. The Narendran Commission, in fact, did a Mandal on Kerala's Hindus. It is, no doubt, a tool aimed at dividing Hindus in the name of reservation. The report of this Commission, submitted to the government on 9 November 2001 has so far been used by the political class as well as minority groups as a powerful weapon to divide the Hindus into elite and subaltern (*savarna* and *avarna*) *jatis*.

The main agents in this pro-Narendran Commission agitation were the pressure groups of the Muslims and the Latin Catholic Christians. The Muslim League is now gearing up to face the threat from Muslim terrorist outfits like the NDF, Solidarity, PDP, etc, within their vote-banks. They want to insulate their outfit from terrorist groups and convert potential sympathizers into solid votes for the time being. In the 2004 parliamentary elections, the Muslim League lost one of its prestigious and traditional seats due to the NDF, even though technically the winner was from the CPM. The growing Muslim terrorist outfits of Kerala, who have no tolerance of other faiths, are on the path of tacit jihad. To make some cleavage in Hindu outfits has become necessary to attain their religious ends. At the same time, the Latin Catholic Christians [backward Christians] are up in arms against Hindu unity, using the camouflage of the Narendran Commission, with Hindu unity moves being criticized openly. The plain fact is that Hindu unity in Kerala is more dangerous to the Church's designs of expanding the frontiers of Christendom in Kerala. Even though the rest of the Christians do not come under the ambit of reservation, they are fiddling the agitation in order to safeguard/fulfill the Church's "third millennium ambitions" —the planting of the cross in Asia—in India.

The main Hindu community leadership (Nairs and Ezhavas) are mutually quarrelling in the battlefield for the leftover bread of OBC reservation. The chief minister had informed the legislative assembly of Kerala during March 2005, that government had

4,86,131 employees and was disbursing Rs 4.8835 billion as salary every month.[3] It is the greatest paradox that aided school and college teachers form part of government employees of Kerala. Of the total government employees, 1,66,119 are aided school teachers.[4] The reservation is applicable only to the posts emerging due to retirement. The OBC share is 10 per cent in rotation to various *jatis*. The foreign remittance to Kerala is three times higher than the plan outlay of the state. The total foreign remittance in 2004 was Rs 184.65 billion. It is seven times what the government receives from the centre as budgetary support or 15 times the earning from the cashew export or19 times the marine export.[5] It is interesting that even in the days of recession, the inflow of foreign remittance to Kerala remained well.

To the Hindus, overseas employment is still a sour grape because of religious reasons. In several other vital sectors like education, industry, and of course, overseas employment, Hindus are marginalized because of the state's excessive minority appeasement. As per the 2001 census, Kerala has 22,58,000 Muslim households. Of this, 34.3 per cent (7,73,465 families) Muslim households have Gulf-employed members.[6] On the other hand, 52,58,631 Hindu households had only 10.4 per cent (5,46,897) overseas employment. In short, one-third of Muslim households in Kerala have a member employed overseas. Similarly, the Dalit and ST community share in overseas employment is very negligible as compared to other communities.[7] Of the 8,51,475 ST households, only 3.3 per cent have the overseas fortune. According to a CDS study in 2004, there were about 18.4 lakh Malayalees with jobs abroad.[8] Their numbers have increased. Among the

18.4 lakh, 43.7 per cent are Muslims, 31.2 per cent are Hindus and 25.1 per cent are Christians.[9]

It is a bare fact that while religious minorities manage 3,340 schools in the state, all Hindu communities together, are in possession of 194 schools only. The Muslim and Christian communities together manage 223 arts and science colleges, against which all Hindu communities together manage only 42 colleges.[10] Out of the 433 professional colleges, only 86 are government-owned, 89 are Hindu-managed while 258 belong to minorities.[11] While all minorities are permitted to impart religious instructions in their respective state-aided educational institutions, this right is denied to Hindu institutions. Hindu students in the minority institutions are not spared and forced to study "moral" classes which inject anti-Hindu ideas amongst the Hindu students in a more sophisticated manner. This is the much-touted "Kerala model of secularist democratic paradigm." As per 1997 statistics, Kerala has 14,200 college teachers; 76 per cent of the college teaching communities hail from minority communities.[12] Recently, the National Minority Education Commission awarded minority status to hundreds of state aided-schools and colleges. The state government was a mere onlooker in this step of NMEC. This change surely makes the Hindus outcastes in state-aided minority institutions.

Similarly, Hindu share in the industry, agriculture and commerce is 28, 24 and 22 per cent respectively. At the same time, Muslim share is 30, 23, 40 per cent and that of Christians 35, 40, 36 per cent respectively.[13] It is not wrong to reach a conclusion that the Hindus of Kerala are the only community in the world, marginalized in a pathetic manner. Hindus lag in several areas, but lead in suicides. Kerala's suicide rate is above the national average, i.e, 30.5 for every lakh. A recent NGO study reveals that 92 per cent of the total suicides are among Hindus, 6.5 per cent among Christians and only 1.5 per cent among Muslims. Insolvency is the main reason of the mass suicides of Kerala Hindus.

Furthermore to convert Kerala into a Dar-ul-Islam, the state government has decided to start Islamic banking in Kerala. Towards this end, the state-owned Kerala State Industrial Development Corporation (KSIDC) had registered an Islamic banking company with a share capital of Rs 10 billion. The government share in the proposed bank is 20 per cent while the remaining comes from jihadists. No one in the state is bothered about this disguised effort to surrender the state's economic control to the pan-Islamic agenda. It was Dr Subramaniam Swamy who came to the rescue of Kerala's Hindus, who have lost relevance in their homeland in the ravages of time, and filed a writ petition challenging the move of the state government in the Kerala High Court. On 5 January 2010, the division bench of the Kerala High Court stayed all further moves and later the Reserve Bank intervened and made it clear that according to existing rules such banks could not be started. If the rest of India is not vigilant, minority-appeasing political parties at the Centre may clear all the hurdles to the idea of Islamic banking in the near future.

The mainstream communist parties of Kerala, after the collapse of Soviet Union and the dramatic changes in China, are eager to woo minorities and the bourgeoisie. Therefore, the ongoing administration in Kerala is functioning basically as anti-Hindu and anti-national. In the line of UPA government at centre (Sachar), the LDF government in Kerala appointed another committee under one of its ministers, Paloli Mohammed, to woo Muslim votes in the coming elections. The committee was constituted with well-known fundamentalist (jihadist) Muslims as members. The committee's recommendations are aimed to socially and economically pressurize the BPL sections in the Hindu society and make religious conversions easier. The state government appointed the committee without any consideration of the current socio-economic status of Muslim women in the all-literate state. The socio-economic disparity between Hindus and the minorities are wide. The lion's share of the BPL in Kerala belongs to the Hindu communities. The commission's justification for the proposal for liberal financial assistance to Kerala's Muslims is that their share in the government service is disproportionate to their ever-increasing population.

As the part of the Paloli Mohammed Committee suggestions, the LDF government granted an additional sop of Rs 1,000 every month as scholarship to Muslim girls. In Kerala, Muslim girls are second to none nowadays. For instance, for the last five years the top scorers in the SSLC, HSC, medical and engineering entrance examinations have been Muslim girls from Malappuram district. The state's women population, irrespective of its religious status, is completely literate. Above all, the latest economic survey conducted by the Marxist Party's intellectual wing revealed that one amongst three Muslim households has a Gulf-employed member. But in the case of Hindus it is only one in ten households. All this proves that the Muslim population of Kerala is in all respects far-ahead of its Hindu counterparts.

Why does a hundred per cent literate state like Kerala have such a small number of Muslims in government jobs? The salary of a school teacher in the state service is Rs 6269, and that of a lower division clerk Rs 6089.[14] Similarly a last grade employee in the state service draws Rs 4300. On the other hand, a Muslim employed abroad sends home Rs 6709 per month. But a Hindu who gets employment abroad is able to send only Rs 4522 to his family and a member hailing from SC community's share is Rs 3066.[15] It is natural that enhanced employment opportunities and better salaries made the Gulf countries the first priority of the Muslims of Kerala. But at the same time, to the Hindu including SCs/STs, a job in the state service is, in monetary terms, better than the Gulf and obviously that would be their first priority. How can a Kerala Muslim then be backward financially?

It is also instructive to examine the landowning pattern of Kerala. Per-household land owning of all Hindus is 69.1 cent, of the Muslims 77.1 cent and in the case of Christians it is 126.4 cents.[16] The Hindu population of Kerala as per the 2001 census is 56.2 per cent. Of them, 5.5 per cent are farmers and 18.3 per cent are farm labours. The Muslim population as per the latest census is 24.7 per cent; among them 6.1 per cent are farmers and 11.8 per cent are farm labourers. The 19.1 per cent Christians are the most blessed as 12.8 per cent of them are farmers and 11.2 per cent agricultural labourers. The numbers of BPL families are also high, 39.3 lakh amongst the Hindus. On the other hand, it is 24.7 lakh and 8.2 lakh respectively amongst Muslims and Christians. Another important disparity between the minorities and the Hindus exists in the case of the possession of habitable houses. 89.7 per cent Muslims live in habitable and *pucca* houses, while in the case of Christians and Hindus it is 80.1 per cent and 83.6 per cent, respectively.[17] When one looks at these economic parameters, the complaint that Muslims are languishing in backwardness is simply ridiculous.

The much-vaunted land reforms of Kerala actually contain the interests of the church. An often-undisclosed fact is that plantations and trust properties were exempted from the land ceiling provisions of the Act, while coconut, pepper and paddy cultivated lands were included. Basically, Hindus are food crop cultivators. Under the pretext of land reform, the government has snatched land from Hindus and let off minorities by resorting to a technical classification of commercial and food crops. Further, in 2005, the government had granted plantation status to cashew cultivating lands.[18] For the last 35 years, cashew-cultivating lands of minorities have been protected from the land ceiling provisions by the state. Thus, this open conspiracy against Hindus and appeasement of minorities is visible even in the matter of land reforms.

In all spheres of socio-economic life, Kerala's Christians and Muslims are far better off than the state's Hindus. Only in numbers of BPL families are Hindus at the top, compared to the minority communities. In the intake of high calorie nutritious food, good living conditions and best education, the minority communities are far ahead of the Hindus. In the field of medical education, 11 medical colleges are owned by the minorities, five by the government, two in the co-operative sector and two under Hindu individual ownership. All the eleven minority-owned institutions are blessed with 'minority institution' status. While minority institutions maintain 1,100 MBBS seats exclusively for students from their communities, government and individual Hindu managements possess only 900 MBBS seats. Out of the 900 seats only 450 are in the general category and are open to all communities. The same is the case with engineering and other paramedical education. Hindu youth's chances have come down to about one-tenth. This disparity is a sufficient testimony to the depth and extent of Hindu marginalization in a state where education decides the destiny of the society.

The alarming growth of Abrahamic religions in India is spreading all over as a scourge. Earlier, it was confined only to Kerala, Goa and the North-East. Proselytism through coercion, allurement and other despicable means is unpretentiously going on in India under the protective shield of vote-bank politics and minority appeasement. The Census of India does not correctly reflect the Christian population. This is because SCs conversion to a non-Indian religion results in the shedding of their SC status. They have to drop all related privileges falling under the statutory dispensations. Therefore, conversions of SCs are a concealed transaction. For instance, on 26 July 2010, Kerala High Court disqualified Kodikunnil Suresh, MP (Cong). He belongs to a second-generation Christian convert, but has represented a reserved parliamentary constituency of Kerala for five terms (1989, 1991, 1996, 1999 and 2009), by producing fake SC certificate. Similarly, several such fake SCs have reached several high positions in the Government of India through such fake transaction in the recent past. Therefore, the periodic Census of India does not reveal the actual Indian Christian population.

The destiny of the microscopic minority of liberal Muslims of Kerala is shrouded in uncertainty. Liberals do not form any vote-bank. Radical Islam (jihadist) is creeping under the protective policy of appeasement. The story of Raihana, a 20-year girl with an engineering degree is a sufficient testimony to the timidity of the contemporary political set-up of Kerala. Raihana hails from Kasaragod, one of the Muslim-dominated districts of Kerala. She eschewed orthodox Muslim clothing and preferred secular attire. The infuriated fundamentalists are now threatening her life. The existing government machinery could not show enough courage to protect her civil rights and she had to secure protection through the high court.[19] History teaches that police protection in Kerala, from KT Jayakrishnan (a UP School teacher and Bharatiya Janata Yuva Morcha president) to Abdul Nasser Madani, hitherto only serve the interest of terrorists. May God protect Raihana!

These appeasement policies of power-mongering politicians of Kerala will bring irrevocable disasters upon the South. The 580 kilometers strategically sensitive but unchecked international border—the state's coastline—is the chief attraction for Muslim fanatics in Kerala and Pakistan's ISI. Since the dawn of history, this international border was protected by its Hindu fishermen communities. Through the ongoing and long conspiracy of proselytism through persecution, allurement and annihilation, Hindu fishermen have been all but eliminated from most parts of the coastal regions of Kerala. The remaining Hindu fisherfolk are not economically or politically strong enough to withstand the challenges posed by the pan-Islamic and evangelical forces in

Kerala. The politicians' competitive sops of pension, scholarships and job reservations going on in Kerala will invite another bloodbath of division along with the annihilation of its remaining Hindu life. Now is the time for reaction throughout India in one voice against these unholy shenanigans of its so-called national political parties, national only in name. I propose a little change to the text of the 19th century call of Swami Vivekananda in the form of the following lines: "These Malabari politicians are to be treated with derision by every patriotic society of India until they end their minority appeasement at the expense of the majority Hindu community."

References

1. *Eakam sat vipra bahuta vatanti-Rig Veda*, Ch III, Suktha 164, Mandala I, Varg 22
2. *EMS's Selected Works*, Mal, Vol. VII, p 356-7
3. *Malayala Manorama*, Kottayam, 19 March 2005
4. Keralam 2000, State Language Institute, Trivandrum, p 908, 909
5. Study by K C Zachria & S Irudayarajan. See: *The New Indian Express*, Kochi, 16 July 2004
6. *Kerala Padanam*, Kerala Sastra Sahitya Parishad, Kozhikode, 2006, p 52
7. *Kerala Padanam*, p 50
8. *Ibid*, Study by K C Zachria & S Irudayarajan
9. *Economic Review* 2004, State Planning Board, February 2005, p 428

10. *Mathrubhumi Daily*, 28 September 2002
11. G K Suresh Babu, Kesari Annual, 2004
12. *Ibid*
13. *Ibid, Matrubhumi*
14. *Kerala Padanam*, op cit, p 65
15. *Kerala Padanam*, op cit, p 52
16. *Kerala Padanam*, op cit, p 54
17. *Kerala Padanam*, op cit, p 48
18. *Business Line*, Kochi, 22 August 2005
19. *The Week*, Kochi, Vol 28, No 40, 29 August 2010, p 54

How Secular is India?

— Devang Nanavati

"India, that is Bharat...*" Thus begins the Constitution of India, and thus would I like to begin my paper. It is this name that I identify my nationality with, one that conjures up in my mind the picture of cultured life of the centuries that have gone by. Since Vedic times, this country, which might have changed its outward appearance today, still remains a venerable motherland, and a land where mutual acceptance and peaceful coexistence have been the way of life. It is in such a Bharat that, even today, unfortunately and painfully, the clarion call of the French Revolution for Liberty, Equality and fraternity still finds an echo. Though this call might

* There has been a major debate on the naming of the country at the time of the framing of the Constitution of the country. Therefore, 'India, that is Bharat' is an indicator of the acknowledgement of the 10000-year old heritage of the land mass called India. These debates have been recorded in the Constitution of India as amended by the Constitution (Ninety-fourth Amendment Act, 2006; Act 44 of 2006 and Act 52 of 2006) (New Delhi: Universal Law Publishing Co. Pvt. Ltd.)

be the basis of 'civilized' society, the very need for it indicates a violation of it. The culture that welcomed other civilizations and ethnicities with open arms now faces a reality where its own existence and constitutional rights seem challenged.

Historically speaking, our country has always been a secular country right from the ancient times (i.e. the Vedic ages). The very essence of the Vedic or Hindu civilization has been founded on the principles of *Sarva Dharma Sadbhav*. Hindus have never believed in a single God, book or dogma. It has been a stream of an unending quest for knowledge leading to the 'Brahman' and the philosophy of the *Atma* and the *Parmatma*. In this quest for the Ultimate Truth, Hinduism has acknowledged plurality and has never restricted itself to one path—religious or otherwise. The *Rig Veda* says: एकम् सद्विप्रा बहुधा वदन्ति (Truth is one, but wise men describe it differently). This has been the philosophy on which the Hindu civilization has been founded and the background on which the Hindu ethos has evolved. Again, the words *Sarva Dharma Sadbhav* suggest an approach of tolerance and understanding of all religions. The *Yajur Veda* states:

मित्रस्यमा चक्षुषा सर्वाणि भूतानि समीक्शन्ताम्
मित्रस्याहं चक्षुषा सर्वाणि भूतानि समीक्षे
मित्रस्य चक्षुषा समीक्शामहे

'May all beings look on me with the eyes of a friend; May I look on all beings with the eyes of a friend. May we look on one another with the eyes of a friend.[1]'

The *Atharva Veda* also states:

जनं विभूति बहुधा विवाचसम
नानाधर्मानं पृथ्वि यथौकसम

This Earth, which accommodates peoples of different persuasions and languages, as in peaceful home—may it benefit all of us.[2]

Again, the *Rig Veda* declares

एकैव मानुषी जाति

All human beings are of one race.[3] This shows that the Vedic civilization has always operated as a secular society which consists of multiplicity in terms of modes of worship and philosophical thought. This is how Buddhism and Jainism also were born, originally from the Vedic traditions and went on to evolve as full-fledged religions or faiths.

The history of India and the religious beliefs of the people of India are one and the same. It is impossible to draw the line of demarcation in the minds of Indians between what are considered "historical facts" and "faith". Thus, the 10,000-year old "Indus" or "Hindu" civilization of India is not only based on the practices, language and culture of the people, but also in the sense of history, unity and common lineage. One of India's leading contemporary thinkers, Arun Shourie writes this in *A Secular Agenda: For Strengthening Our Country, For Welding It*:

"India has been seen as one and its people have had a common way of life for thousands of years. It is not just that its history is that old, as it is in the case of the Greeks. It is a continuous history. The way of life today—the people's beliefs and practices—can be traced directly and by a chain of unsevered links to what was taught and practised thousands of years ago. Indeed, the wail of its denouncers—that we have not shed our past—testifies to the age and continuity of the tradition.

The land, its mountains and rivers are venerated in the *Rig* and the *Atharva Vedas* in the very way they are in Bankim's *Vande Matram* or Tagore's *Jana-Gana-Mana*. The land is celebrated and venerated from those ancient times not just because of the great bounties it bestows on us but because it is seen as the *Karma-Bhumi*, because it has been the place where the greatest souls revered by the people have performed great deeds—of nobility, or valour and where they have attained the deepest insights. The *Mahabharata* and the *Ramayana* describe warring states but they are the epics of one people."[4]

Hinduism, thus is a civilization, and its history is an integral part of all who call themselves Indians. The *Vedas* and other ancient texts are not only Hindu texts but also historical texts and Indian texts. The culture and the texts teach as well as practice openness and plurality.

Against such a history of accommodativeness and accord, our national reality today is built up on a threat of anti-secularism that faces any religious expression from the majority, an appeasing of the minority for vote-bank politics, and the danger of losing that historical Bharat which flourished on Hindu catholicity. This paper will go on to show how, on the one hand, the same Constitution (that was adopted by the country's pre-independence leaders, many of whom had a clear Vedic bent of mind, were scholars themselves, and believers in the Hindu roots of India*)

---

* Dr Radhakrishnan, the second President of India, quotes extensively from the ancient Indian scriptures in his speeches. The debate on the drafting of the Constitution of India also indicates the Hindu scholarship of great minds like Seth Govind Das, Shri Kallur Subba Rao, Shri Kamalapati Tripathi and Shri Hargovind Pant. The Constitutient Assembly Debates: Official Report. (New Delhi: Jaico Art India, 1999)

that has been inspired by, what is considered the most successful democracy in the world—the United States of America—does not accept the religious foundations on which the country stands. On the other hand, as this paper compares India's 'secularism' with other supposedly secular countries, it will also illustrate the fact that justice is not done to the Hindu majority in the country in ignoring/rejecting the historical Hindu lineage/heritage/descent, of all Indians. In conclusion, the paper will question the methods and means used by parties in power to create a so-called 'secular' country wherein the very definition of secularism is flawed, due to the rejection of the heart of Hinduism in the people of India.

My premise is that there has been a concerted effort to destroy the values of India's civilization and cultural nationalization in the name of 'secularism'. There is no argument that the word 'Hindu', signifying the people who lived since ancient times on the banks of the river Sindhu, is synonyms with the word 'India'*. Yet, if one tries to be a practising Hindu today, the person is dubbed either as communal or fascist and certainly non-secular. In India, if one tries to gauge the meaning of a secular individual, the common conclusion of the so-called 'secular' imagination is that one needs to break all ties with the past, claim to have a religion only secondarily, have no continuity with a 10,000-year old and still surviving civilization. It is assumed—falsely—that only this would make one truly secular. It is this misinterpretation of the word secularism which has given rise to a feeling of separatism in India—a separatism that arises from disconnecting with one's past

* The Constituent Assembly Debates: Official Report. (New Delhi: Jaico Art India, 1999) 1686

and denying one's roots. As a result of this faulty understanding of the term, there emanate deficient and flawed perceptions/views not only in matters of great national importance, but also in basic, constitutional individual rights and privileges.

A direct consequence of this self-same misinterpretation of the concept of secularism is the problem of minority appeasement. It is common knowledge that the Indian Constitution categorically claims all religions and religious beliefs as equally privileged (Articles 26 to 30). Now, if this is the law of the land, then why do certain minorities claim more privileges than the majority population? And if any privileges are given to the followers of Hinduism, why would they be perceived as non-secular or fascist? First of all, as stated earlier, Hinduism or Hindutva is a culture that has been in existence, since thousands of years. It is a civilization which cannot be narrowly defined as a religion. If everyone living in India can trace their lineage back to their ancestors, they are certain to find at least one Hindu root, irrespective of their religion! This is because Hinduism is a way of life, as the cliché goes, that welcomed all 'religions'. If this is so, then logically speaking, everyone is a Hindu, and therefore, need not have any minority privilege. Even the father of the nation believed in having no special categories when he stated:

"...the poisonous favouritism of foreign rule was dead and gone. Merit should be the sole test. In a well-ordered society there should be no minority.*"

---

* Rakesh Sinha cites this quote in his article "Hindutva Movement and Politics" in Hindutva in Present Context: Proceedings of the seminar on "Hindutva in Present Context." Eds. Vijay Chauthaiwale, Shreekant Katdare, Purujit Saiyed. (Ahmedabad: Bhartiya Vichar Manch, 2010) 303

Further, why should any advantage given to the majority be construed only as non-secular? Just as a religious advantage can be given to a minority, it can also be given to a majority in a country that claims to practise religious equality.

The Amarnath controversy illustrates this point best. At the time of the 2008 Jammu & Kashmir assembly elections, the state government of Jammu and Kashmir decided to allot 100 acres of land in a place called Batal in Kashmir to the Amarnath Shrine Board (Public Trust) on lease, to create infrastructural facilities for Hindu pilgrims going on the annual Amarnath Yatra. Located thousands of feet above sea level, Batal is a dense forest area, completely unusable for any purpose, including agriculture, and not useful for habitation of human beings or animals. In fact, the living conditions are so harsh in this area that it is practically inaccessible to humans for nine months out of twelve. However, separatist elements in Jammu and Kashmir, sponsored and instigated by Pakistan launched a vicious agitation against this allocation of land, branding this action of the state government as anti-secular and termed it as an attempt to promote the Hindu religion. Unfortunately, the state regime buckled under pressure and cancelled the legitimate allotment; in fact, it even went on to dissolve the Amarnath Shrine Board itself. In a country where people belonging to the Islamic faith are given magnanimous subsidies to go on the Haj pilgrimage every year, for which massive largesse is doled out by the government–like specially established airport terminals and counters at most airports across the country–why should a proportionately small facility not be provided to the people going on a Hindu pilgrimage? In the name of 'secularism', does the major faith of the country have to suffer the adversities of nature and the whims of the rulers of the day in order to worship at a shrine? Even by the bigoted definition of the so-called secularists, if we were to apply the provisions of Article 29, Hindus should have the right to maintain their culture and conserve the same in the state of Jammu and Kashmir where they are in a minority. Yet, we can clearly see how vested interests ensure that 'secularism' is used as a tool not to unite but to disintegrate the country and society. This vote-bank politics will slowly but surely destroy the actual unity and the fabric of integrity of India by camouflaging itself under the very provision that was intended to strengthen the unity and integrity of the nation. In fact, this is a violation of the constitutional right of an individual—the freedom to manage religious affairs and the right to establish and maintain institutions for religious and charitable purposes. (Article 26)

Another such example is the controversy regarding our national song—Bankim Chandra Chatopadhyay's "*Vande Mataram.*" This song which inspired patriotic fervor since pre-independence days has been condemned as anti-secular. This controversy, raised by some Muslims, alleges that the singing of *Vande Mataram* is against the tenets of Islam and that its verses have no place in secular India. As recently as 2009, the Deobandis issued a fatwa to Muslims in India against the singing of the country's national song—'*Vande Mataram*'.

The drive to appease the "minorities" (read Muslims) has been so strong that even though the Constitution has accepted *Vande Mataram* as a national song, it did so only after truncating the original poem and its verses so as not to offend the minorities.

It is however, interesting to note that the fatwa issued in 2009 is against even this truncated version. The song, which was a symbol and torchbearer of India's struggle for independence is to be erased from our memories in the name of 'secularism'. The argument presented is that one doesn't have to sing *Vande Mataram* in order to be nationalistic or patriotic.

These are some illustrations of India's practice of a misinterpreted idea of 'secularism'. It is easy to blame the presence of anti-secularism on the British. Historically speaking, it is true that the East India Company that brought British rule to India eventually divided communities that used to live in perfect harmony and peaceful coexistence. However, in the proclamation described as "the Magna Carta of The Indian People," Queen Victoria herself has stated the totally secular spirit of her realm:

"Firmly relying ourselves on the truth of Christianity and acknowledging with gratitude the solace of religion, we disclaim alike the right and the desire to impose our convictions on any of our subjects. We declare it to be our royal will and pleasure that none any wise favoured, none molested or disqualified by reason of their religious faith and observance; but that all shall alike enjoy the equal and impartial protection of the law, and we do strictly charge and enjoin those who may be in authority under us that they abstain from all interference with the religious belief or worship or any of our subjects on pain of our highest displeasure.

And it is our further will that so far as may be, our subjects of whatever race or creed be freely and impartially admitted to offices in our service, the duties of which they may be qualified by their education, ability and integrity, duly to discharge.

We know and respect the feelings of attachment with which the natives of India regard the land inherited by them from their ancestors and we desire to protect them in all rights connected therewith subject to the equitable demands of the state and we will do that generally in framing and administering the law, due regard be paid to the ancient rights and customs of India.[5]"

In spite of her British Christian background, this proclamation of the Queen shows the spirit of secularism even in the British Empire. It is this spirit that went hand in hand with the openness of the civilization and culture of India.

Despite the tall proclamations of religious and individual freedom in the Constitution of India, the political appeasement of the minorities which created divides, and the political complacency of the administration, compel us to look into the very framing of this Constitution.

The Indian Constitution has had the advantage of borrowing from the modern Constitutions of the world. The concept of Liberty, Equality and Justice were borrowed from the French. Similarly, we have also relied heavily on the American Constitution, which is considered one of the most successful democratic constitutions of the world. The first amendment of the American Constitution stating that "Congress shall make no law respecting and establishing of religion, or prohibiting the free exercise thereof," is the basis of the Secular philosophy of the American Constitution and is used, in Jefferson's words, for "Building a Wall of separation between the Church and State." It essentially connotes that the state shall have no religion, nor will it pass any law which aids one religion or prefers one religion over another. In other words, it meant that the state shall be neutral in matters of religion. At home, Justice K Ramaswamy of our own Supreme Court stated this in the case of S R Bommai versus Union of India.[6]

"Freedom of faith and religion is an integral part of social structure. Such freedom is not a bounty of the state but constitutes the very foundation on which the state is erected. Human liberty sometimes means to satisfy the human needs in ones own way. … Democratic society realizes the folly of the vigour of the religious practices in society. Strong religious consciousness not only narrows the vision but hampers the rule of law. The Founding Fathers of the Constitution, therefore, gave unto themselves "We people of India," the Fundamental Rights and Directive Principles of State Policy to establish an egalitarian social order for all sections of society in the supreme law of the land itself. Thought the concept of "secularism" was not expressly engrafted while making the Constitution, its sweep, operation and visibility are apparent from the fundamental rights, the directive principles and their related provisions. It was made explicit by amending the preamble of the Constitution in the 42nd Amendment Act. The concept of secularism, of which religious freedom is the foremost, appears to visualize not only the subject of God but also an understanding between man and man. Secularism in the Constitution is not anti-God….The concept of the secular State is, therefore, essential for successful working of the democratic form of government. There can be no democracy if anti-secular forces are allowed to work dividing followers of different religious faiths."[7]

This shows that even in the highest court of India, secularism in the true sense meant the freedom to practice any religious faith.

While taking into account the importance of religion in the life of a citizen, the court decrees at the same time, that a secular state is one in which there is also an understanding between man and man. If this is the explanation of secularism given by the Supreme Court of India, then how do we explain the Islamic fatwa on *Vande Mataram* or the dissolution of the Amarnath Shrine Board? Some of the provisions of Constitution in this regard are as follows:

Article 26: Freedom to manage religious affairs–Subject to public order, morality and health, every religious denomination or any section thereof shall have the right.

1. to establish and maintain institutions for religious and charitable purposes;
2. to manage its own affairs in matters of religion;
3. to own and acquire movable and immovable property; and
4. to administer such property in accordance with law.

Article 27: Freedom as to payment of taxes for promotion of any particular religion

No person shall be compelled to pay taxes, the proceeds of which are specifically appropriated in payment of expenses for the promotion of maintenance of any particular or religious denomination.

Article 28: Freedom as to attendance at religious instruction or religious worship in certain educational institutions

1. No religious instruction shall be provided in any educational institution wholly maintained out of State funds.
2. Nothing in the clause (1) shall apply to an educational institution which is administered by the State but has been established under any endowment or trust which requires that

religious instruction shall be imparted in such institution.

3. No person attending any educational institution recognized by the State or receiving aid out of State funds shall be required to take part in any religious instruction that may be imparted in such institution or to attend any religious worship that may be conducted in such institution or in any premises attached thereto unless such person or, if such person is a minor, his guardian has given his consent thereto.

Article 29 Protection of interest of minorities

1. Any section of the citizens residing in the territory or any part thereof having a distinct language, script or culture of its own shall have the right to conserve the same.
2. No citizen shall be denied admission into any educational institutions maintained by the State or receiving aid out of State funds on grounds only of religion, race, caste, language or any of them.

Article 30: Right of minorities to establish and administer educational institutions

1. All minorities, whether based on religion or language shall have the right to establish and administer educational institutions of their choice. [(1A) In making any law providing for the compulsory acquisition of any property of an educational institution established and administered by a minority, referred to in clause (1) the State shall ensure that the amount fixed by or determined under such law for the acquisition of such property is such as would not restrict or abrogate the right guaranteed under that clause]
2. The State shall not, in granting aid to educational institutions,

discriminate against any educational institution on the ground that it is under the management of a minority, whether based on religion or language.

In contrast with all the examples of India's misinterpreted perception of secularism, consider these examples from the United States of America. These examples are taken because as mentioned earlier, the concept of secularism in our Constitution has been influenced by the first amendment to the US Constitution*. Three cases that came before the US Supreme Court in connection with the first amendment of the US Constitution are relevant in making a point here. The first case–Emerson vs Board of Education, 330 US 1 (1947)—was regarding the facility of transportation for a group of children going to a parish school in New Jersey. This school would impart religious education to children, and instead of offering free transport services, would reimburse transport expenses to the parents of the children. The argument against this school was that the First Amendment prohibits the promotion of religious faith, and therefore the reimbursement is a violation of the Amendment. However, the court decreed that the reimbursement was not a violation of the Amendment because the transport was provided to children to receive a certain education—religious or otherwise. So, the judge used the argument of child benefit to

---

* The opening words of the Constitution's First Amendment of the United States of America are "Congress shall make no law respecting an establishment of religion, or prohibiting the free exercise thereof." (The Supreme Court on church and State, New York, Oxford: Oxford University Press, 1988) and the Indian Constitution Articles 25, 26, 27 and 28 claim the right to religious freedom.

support his judgment and permitted the free transport facility to the children to go to the religious school in public interest.

The second case is that of Marsh vs Chamber*. In this case, there was a controversy pertaining to the Legislature of Nebraska. The controversy was whether the position and function of the Chaplain—a clergyperson—who was paid by the State for opening each of the Legislative days, was an infringement of the Establishment Clause of the US Constitution. In other words, the alleged claim was that opening the Legislature with a prayer was a violation of the first amendment of the US Constitution. The US Supreme Court, while coming to the conclusion that the above action was not violative of the secular establishment clause of the US Constitution, speaking through Chief Justice Berger held the following:

"This unique history leads us to accept the interpretation of the first amendment draftsman, which was no real threat to the establishment clause arising from a practice of prayer similarly to that now challenged. We conclude that Legislative prayer presents no more potential for establishment than the provision of school transportation beneficial grants for higher education, or tax exemptions for religious organizations."

The judgment of the court goes on to say that

"We do not agree that evidence of opposition to a measure weakens the force of the historical argument: indeed, it infuses it with power by demonstrating that the subject was considered carefully and the action not taken thoughtlessly, by force of long tradition and without regard to the problems posed by a pluralistic society."

---

* 463 US 783 (1983)

It further states

"In the light of the unambiguous and unbroken history of more than 200 years, there can be no doubt that the practice of opening legislative sessions with prayer has become part of the fabric of our society. To invoke divine guidance on a public body entrusted with making the laws is not, in these circumstances, an "establishment" of religion or a step toward establishment: it is simply a tolerable acknowledgement of beliefs widely held among the people of this country...." (Alley, 302-303)

The third case—Lynch vs Donnelly, 465 US 668 (1984) is that regarding the display of Christmas symbols in public places. The argument against these purely religious displays on public property was that they violated the first amendment. The ruling of the court was thus:

"No significant segment of our society and no institution within it can exist in a vacuum or in total or absolute isolation from all the other parts, much less from the government. "It has never been thought either possible or desirable to enforce a regime of total separation...." Nor does the Constitution require complete separation of church and state; it affirmatively mandates accommodation, not merely tolerance, of all religions, and forbids hostility toward any. Anything less would require the "callous indifference" we have said was never intended by the Establishment Clause. Indeed, we have observed, such hostility would bring us into "conflict with our national tradition as embodied in the First Amendment's guaranty of the free exercise of religion." (Alley, 320)

The Court also stated pointedly "We are a religious people whose institutions presuppose a Supreme Being." (Alley, 321) and further gave other examples of the religious heritage of America by referring to the national motto that is mandated in the currency: "In God We Trust" and the pledge to the American flag: "One nation under God." Moreover, the court stated there were many examples of masterpieces with religious messages like the Last Supper, the Crucifixion, Moses with the Ten Commandments etc which are displayed at many places, and which have long been a source of worship and meditation.

Thus, it can be seen that even in a country where secularism is supposedly practiced to the hilt and where the founding fathers of America wanted to create a wall of separation between the Church and State, the history, traditions and the beliefs of the majority of the people have been taken into consideration in determining the scope and meaning of secularism. Of course, secularism cannot become a positive religion in itself. At its best, it is neutrality towards matters of religious faith. However, under the cover of this term, we cannot ignore a civilization and its historical traditions.

Conclusion

The concept of secularism straitjacketed into a formula. "The Establishment Clause like the due process clause is not a precise, detailed provision in a legal court capable of ready application. The purpose of the establishment clause "was to state an objective, not to write a statute." (Alley, 323)

Then, what would be permissible or impermissible under the term 'secularism'? In other words, how is secularism to be defined and determined while taking into consideration the cultural and civilization history of the country, so as not to cause any religion or culture any impediments in manner or form? Can we even imagine our country wherein parliament sessions were to begin with a recitation from *Bhagwad Gita* by a priest, who would be paid by the government? The debates on and off the media would most certainly dub this act as "communal," "fascist" and even "anti-national." Why should a Hindu prayer, religious expression, cultural practice or mode of behaviour in a country with a Hindu majority threaten the minorities of the country? And if it does, should they be protected under the garb of 'secularism'? With these questions, I wish to challenge the current misuse of the concept of secularism in order to indicate the path forward.

The Constitution is a transient document and needs to be understood in its spirit, as well as in the context of the times. Though, it does state a protection of the minorities, it declares more importantly, religious freedom for all citizens. Therefore, if a minority community arranging/organizing a religious expression is not termed as "anti-secular," then there is absolutely no justification for the majority community doing the same to be branded as such. The spirit of the Constitution suggests that the religious expression of the majority was already taken for granted and need not be argued at all. Today, however, minority appeasement arising out of vote-bank politics sidelines the majority population of India and creates a situation which deliberately confuses the cultural expression of Hindus with religious worship.

Secondly, if all religions are to be treated equally according to the Constitution of India, subsidies allowed to minorities like the Haj pilgrims should also be allowed to the majority culture. The

Amarnath Shrine Board, though not a subsidy, was a beneficiary organization for the Hindus and must be allowed to remain so. The land allocated for Hindu pilgrims is equivalent to a Haj subsidy and should continue as such.

Thirdly, Article 26 of the Constitution allows freedom of religious practice. However, if that freedom is misused to create anti-national or divisive sentiment, the State needs to intervene and regulate this freedom. On the one hand, the State has taken over the regulation of the trusts running important Hindu temples in the country like the Tirupati temple, the Somnath temple, the Dwarka temple etc, but on the other hand, minority institutions like schools, madrassas etc are unregulated and un-supervised. This again exposes the divisiveness and open bias of the attitude of those in power.

Finally, as in the cases of the United States of America, the State should take into account the fact that any expression of religious/cultural/historical/traditional practice, in actuality and in spirit, does no other community any harm. In fact, it is natural human behaviour and a basic premise that is and must be taken for granted under any laws. Take for instance, how the people in India celebrate the festivals of Diwali, Holi and others. If this misconception of secularity is pushed forward in this way, it might result in justifying these self-same celebrations too. If, at every step, the majority population of the country needs to justify an expression of tradition and culture, then the term 'secular in itself' cannot be justified. Hence, my question: How neutral is secular India today? In fact, how 'secular' is India?

References

1. Supreme Court cases 1994 Volume 6, p 399
2. *Ibid*
3. Supreme Court cases 1994 Volume 6, p 400
4. Shourie, 1993, p 9
5. 100 significant pre-Independence speeches
6. Case of S R Bommai versus Union of India: p163 para178
7. Supreme Court cases 1994 Volume 3, p 163, para 178

Demons Haunt God's Own Country

— Hari S Kartha

Kerala, often described as "God's Own Country", and rightly so, has been India's crucible of many experiments—political, economic, social and educational. The unique and unparalleled achievements of the state in life expectancy, healthcare and education, right since pre-independence days have been hailed by economists all over the world as the Kerala Model of Development. The state attracted international attention by electing to power a communist regime for the first time, thereby proving Karl Marx wrong. But when the followers of Marx, in the then government headed by E M Sankaran Namboodiripad committed wrongs, the first-ever elected communist regime was brought down by a popular uprising named 'the Liberation Struggle'. Kerala was also the first Indian state to experiment with coalition politics. In social renaissance, the princely state of Travancore, which later merged with Kerala, crossed a major milestone by the Temple Entry Proclamation when the then Maharaja had thrown open temples to the so-called untouchables. It has been a series of experiments—often good, occasionally bad and sometimes even ugly.

Kerala is a big bundle of paradoxes. The communists who captured power through the ballot in the fifties could never come to power on their own afterwards. The state, which takes pride in being the most politically conscious, has perhaps the maximum number of political parties, all having enjoyed power, barring BJP. Intriguingly, the Congress and its allies were voted back to power with a thumping majority in the general elections that followed the Emergency, demolishing the myth that the state is politically conscious. The common minimum programme of coalitions that have been in power, led by both the Left and the centrists, has been to remain in power at the expense of political and ideological principles. Little wonder that the land which gave birth to Shri Adi Sankara and Advaita also produced and nurtured a Red Sankara, Sankaran Namboodiripad, also from the very same community.

Alarmingly, Kerala is today the breeding ground for fundamentalists and terrorists. Any terrorist attack or serial bomb blast, anywhere in the country, is likely to have a Kerala connection. Besides breeding fundamentalists, terrorist outfits have also identified Kerala as the safest training ground for their cadres.

All the ills of Kerala, be it on the political, economic, agricultural, industrial, educational or social fronts can be traced to minorityism, which has been the dominant force behind every political conspiracy in the state, even before independence. In the erstwhile Travancore princely state under the Maharajah, the Christian church conspired against the then Dewan Sir C P

Ramaswami Iyer. Paradoxically, it was the Leftists who unknowingly became a tool in the hands of the church, in physically attacking the Dewan at a public function in the state capital, prompting him to leave the state for ever. With the formation of Kerala and replacement of the Raja's reign by the popular regime, the church spearheaded the Liberation Struggle that brought down the first-ever elected communist government. The communist movement in Kerala—at least initially—was in fact, a political Hindu backlash against the then Christian-dominated Congress. It is significant in this context that leaders of Hindutva movement in the country, including Swantantryaveer Vinayak Damodar Savarkar and Shri Guruji Golwalkar had openly criticized the Liberation Struggle and condemned the dismissal of the then EMS Namboodiripad ministry in Kerala by the Centre. It was minorityism that was responsible for the departure of the last Dewan as well as the state's first Chief Minister. Minorityism continues to set the agenda and minority communities continue to dictate terms in Kerala, irrespective of the political complexion of the government.

Perhaps nowhere else in India is vote-bank politics as glaring and dangerous as in Kerala. Little wonder that the Muslim League, which was dubbed by late Pundit Jawaharlal Nehru as "the dead horse" started galloping again in Kerala. This was the result of the Congress and the CPM vying with each other to politically patronize and promote Muslim League since the sixties. Despite stiff opposition from several quarters, a Muslim majority district of Malappuram was created by EMS. Namboodiripad when he became Chief Minister for the second time. Earlier, it was the Muslim communalism of the Muslim League which was the state's bane, while today it is the Islamic fundamentalism of Jamait-e-Islami, the Popular Front and the Peoples Democratic Party that stalks Kerala. With the emergence of these new aggressive outfits, the Muslim League has also been pushed to pursue extremist policies. Muslim League leaders, even when they are ministers, refuse to light the lamp as part of the traditional style of inauguration of any public function. Cinema houses are set afire in Muslim strongholds as part of Talibanization. Even the statue of Thunchath Ezhuthachan, the father of Malayalam language and literature has been kept in wraps for several years at his birthplace, as Muslims refuse to allow its installation at a public place. At the same time, an award initially instituted by the late Maharajah for outstanding contributions to Malayalam literature was cancelled by the present Left Democratic Front government, as according to the government, an award in the name of Sri Padmanabha was "anti-secular". But the same government had no qualms in honouring the virulent anti-Hindu M F Hussain with the Ravi Varma award. Arabic gets special consideration and promotion while Sanskrit faces step-motherly treatment by the state. Mullahs and Moulavis enjoy government pensions and other welfare measures while *poojaris* in temples starve in poverty. Minorities get protection and concessions, even in revenue reforms. No less an economist than the late K N Raj had pointed out that the much hailed land reforms by the state government never covered plantations owned by minorities. Precisely, what is being witnessed in Kerala is the nauseating competitive minority appeasement by the two warring fronts, LDF and UDF.

This is exactly what facilitated a unanimous resolution by

the Kerala Assembly a few years back, demanding that the PDP chief Abdul Nasser Madani, accused in the Coimbatore bomb blast case (which claimed more than 60 lives) be unconditionally released from a Tamil Nadu prison. Never in legislative history has there been such a demand by a house of people's representatives. When Madani was finally released three years back, the ruling LDF organized a grand public reception for this Islamic terrorist don in Thiruvananthapuram, also attended by four ministers. Even in the self-styled secular political parties, minorityism holds complete sway. Not only the erstwhile Diwan and the communist chief minister, but Congress strongman and the state's chief minister on many occasion (the late) K Karunakran too lost his chief minister's chair because of the minorities' ire. Whether it is the CPM-led Left Democratic Front or the Congress-led United Democratic Front that is in power, all key portfolios are always held only by representatives of minority communities, often by the church-sponsored Kerala Congress or the Muslim League. The bureaucracy is controlled by well-organized minority communities. Right from schools to universities, these non-Hindu minorities have a monopoly. Economic activity is controlled by minority communities, be it in industry, trade or agriculture. Of late, they have begun making forays even in land ownership. Properties owned by Hindus are being purchased offering fancy prices. On the one hand is "love jihad" and on the other this new land jihad has started cropping up. Alarmingly, a concerted but sinister attempt by Muslims is on, to buy up the entire land surrounding important Hindu temples like Guruvayoor. Business today in Sabarimala, the famous hill shrine, is Muslim-dominated. The attempt is obviously to ensure that even Lord Guruvayoorappa and Lord Ayyappa are at the mercy of the Muslims.

The rudest shock came hardly two months back when a college professor of a Christian management college, was attacked on his way back from church on a Sunday and his right hand chopped off, by a gang of Muslim terrorists using an axe, in the presence of his sister and aged mother on the public road in broad daylight. The charge against the professor was that he had referred to one Mohammed in a question paper. Making life further miserable for the Professor (who is a Christian), the Christian management of the college, as directed by the church daises has dismissed him from service. The daises' indirect approval of the barbarous act by the Muslim bigots seems to have more to it than meets the eye. The million-dollar question posed by this twin action is: are the two minority communities hand-in-glove in Kerala? In the last three years more than a score of Hindu youths have been killed by the Muslim extremists in different parts of the state. Not only non-Muslims, even a Muslim Scholar, Abdul Maoulavi was butchered and buried somewhere with no trace. Kerala, hitherto hailed as "God's Own Country" is today being haunted by demons.

It has already come from the horse's mouth that efforts are underway to convert Kerala into a Muslim majority state within the next twenty years. CPM politburo member and Chief Minister V S Achuthanandan's unambiguous recent disclosure to the media in Delhi that Muslin fundamentalist organizations were planning to ensure that Kerala is a Muslim majority state within two decades, not surprisingly, aroused a controversy. Prior to that the

Cardinal of Kochi, Mar Varkey Vithayathil also had told in a press interview that the church had to be on guard, as at the present rate of population growth the state will be Muslim majority in another twenty years. In a sharp twist of irony, the general apprehension of the Hindus in Kerala is now being endorsed by a communist chief minister and the Christian church as well.

Naga Terrorists in League with Politicians

— Jagdamba Mall

Prior to Independence, it was the brave Angami communities of Khonoma, Mezoma and Kekrüma in Nagaland who fought British rule and Christian proselytizing, an-often untold story of India's North-East. The Chakhesang Nagas of Thevopisumi village fought against Christian conversion and the church-sponsored Naga National Council (NNC) led by A Z Phizo—who demanded complete secession from Bharatvarsh. Haipou Jadonang—a Rongmei Naga from Manipur who led a strong resistance to British expansion and missionary menace, was hanged on 29 August 1931. Rani Gaidinliu—then a girl of 16 years led the movement called Zeliangrong Heraka Movement to protect the sovereignty of the country and the indigenous Hindu faith. Even A Z Phizo, who hailed from Khonoma village, assisted the Indian National Army (INA) led by Netaji Subhash Chandra Bose in the Kohima theatre during the Second World

War to defeat the British. However, the early British inroads into the Naga Hills and tribes enabled them to push American and British Christian missionaries into Nagaland, under their army protection and support of their regime in India. Forced conversions to Christianity and expansion of British imperial rule went hand-in-hand. After their "grand success" in dividing the country to create East and West Pakistan, the British picked up Phizo and NNC cohorts with the long-term aim of carving out a separate Christian country in Northeast Bharat.

The British rulers first employed Christian missionaries to convert Nagas and then instigated the converted Nagas (Phizo and NNC militants) to start a Middle Age-style inquisition against those Nagas who refused to convert to Christianity and support British policy after 1947. The aim was to establish a "Christian solidarity" with the US and the UK, with the American and British Baptist Christian Church taking the initiative for the formation of a Christian Sovereign Nagaland. Phizo who supported Army of Subhash Chandra Bose and fought against the British, later joined the British bandwagon, after conversion to Christianity, and waged a war on Bharatvarsh to secede from the country and started Christian inquisitions in support of the Christian crusade, to convert all Nagas to please his British masters. Anybody who expressed a different opinion was brutally killed. NNC and church were all the same. Overnight, churches opened in even remote areas, and became shelters for the guerillas of NNC.

Missionaries acted as informers against army movements and against those Nagas who did not support NNC uprising and Christian inquisition jointly operated by the NNC and the Church. This was the reason that Rani Gaidinliu, a Naga freedom fighter, and her Zeliangrong Heraka (Hindus) movement were the prime target of both. They (NNC and Church) were after Rani Gaidinliu. British missionary Michael Scott became a friend, philosopher and guide of Phizo and NNC insurgency. This British priest supplied lethal weapons packed in Red Cross boxes to NNC terrorists. The Church formed several NGOs which played host to NNC guerillas and their Christian crusade. The government of India, under Jawaharlal Nehru failed to pay requisite attention to this conspiracy against the country by NNC and Church combined.

The Crown Colony Plan

The British had a Crown Colony plan–a buffer state under British rule, in independent Bharatvarsh by detaching it from the Siliguri corridor. When this could not happen at the time of secession of both wings of Pakistan (East and West) in 1947, they employed NNC guerillas and the Church organization to realize their dream of a buffer state in the Naga Hills, which could be a military base for America and Britain because of NE's strategic location in the midst of Hindu Bharat, Communist China and Muslim East Pakistan (now Bangladesh). With their long experience in the Divide and Rule policy, the marauders in London crushed and killed all Naga leaders who opposed annexation of Naga areas with British Crown and conversion of Nagas through force, fraud and proselytizing. This they accomplished through the NNC, Church and several Naga NGOs created under the supervision of the British plotters planted in Church organizations. Naga Club and Naga Hoho were two such NGOs, who were master campaigners and expert educators of NNC and the Church agenda amongst the Naga public. When GOI wanted to arrest Phizo for his anti-national activities, he silently escaped to London where he spent a royal life till his death in 1990, hosted by British Church organization under the supervision of Michael Scott and Billy Graham, a rabid anti-Hindu evangelist.

Division of NNC

In 1975 during the Emergency, the NNC signed the Shillong Accord, accepting the Constitution of the country. A few hard-core militants defected from the NNC under the leadership of Muivah (Tangkhul Naga), Isak Chishi Swu (Sema Naga) and S S Khaplang (Hemi Naga) because of ideological differences. They went to China for military training and formed the National Socialist Council of Nagaland (NSCN) in 1980 under the influence of Chinese Communism. This outfit again split into two–the NSCN (IM) under the leadership of Isak Chishi Swu and Muivah and NSCN (K) led by S S Khaplang. Two years later, NNC was also divided into two–NNC (Adino) and NNC (Yanthan) after the death of Phizo in 1990. Adino is the daughter of Phizo and Khadao Yanthan (Lotha Naga) is the former private secretary of Phizo. All the four factions started killing each other in the war of supremacy, even after the conciliatory role played by many NGOs like Naga Hoho, Nagaland Baptist Council of Churches (NBCC), Naga Student Federation (NSF), Naga Mother Association (NMA), Naga People's Movement for Human Rights (NPMHR), and Naga Club (now dormant) etc. Several masked

NGOs are registered under the country's laws and also under the Foreign Contribution Regulation Act 1976 with a declared aim of serving the society in the field of economic uplift, hygiene, medical care education and HIV/AIDS. These NGOs are receiving uncountable money from their foreign masters through hawala and also through all the possible legal and illegal means. In return, they fund rebel organizations for purchasing lethal weapons and are also involved in drug, liquor and child trafficking in Nagaland and neighbouring states.

There are other NGOs which work under the garb of student organizations, youth organizations, tribal hohos (apex bodies), civil organizations and human rights organizations, openly receiving money from state governments. In other words, these organizations are nourished by the state government and foreign funding agencies inimical to our nation. Thus, the State Government of Nagaland is aiding and abetting Naga insurgency.

Prominent Native NGOs in league with NSCN (IM)

1. Nagaland Baptist Council of Churches (NBCC)
2. Council of Nagalim Baptist Churches (CNBC)
3. Naga Student Federation (NSF) and its affiliated tribal student bodies.
4. Naga Hoho (NH)
5. Naga People's Movement for Human Rights (NPMHR)
6. Naga Mother Association (NMA)
7. Catholic Churches in Nagaland
8. Islamic organizations in league with ISI
9. United Naga Council, Manipur (UCM)

10. All Naga Students Association of Manipur (ANSAM)
11. Jirsong Asong, Diphu
12. Human Rights Alert, Manipur
13. Concerned Senior Citizens Forum, Nagaland. This is a newly-born NGO—a front organization of NSCN (IM). It is engaged in awareness campaign for mobilizing support of Nagas of Nagaland in favour of Muivah and his Tangkhul lieutenants by organizing a seminar on Indigenous Peoples' Right in line with UN declaration in November 2007.
14. Naga Women Union Manipur (NWUM)
15. Assam Watch
16. All Party Hurriyat Conference (APHC)
17. World Kashmir Freedom Movement (WKFM)
18. Jammu-Kashmir Liberation Front (JKLF)
19. British Sikh Federation (BSF)
20. Dal Khalsa
21. Global Watch Prayer Ministry (GWPM)
22. Shepoumaramth Rights Watch (SRW)
23. Human Rights Watch–New Delhi
24. People's Union for Civil Liberties (PUCL), New Delhi
25. Other Media, New Delhi
26. Naga People's Forum, New Delhi
27. Commonwealth Policy Studies, Delhi
28. Tirap Changlong Human Rights Organization (TICHRO) PO-Miao, Changlong, Arunachal Pradesh. Miao is the Bishop's headquarter of Catholic Church.
29. International Organization for Human Rights Protection, Nagaland Unit (IOHRP-N): This is another Human Rights body formed recently in Nagaland.

Efforts are being made to spread its tentacles in all the eleven districts of Nagaland and other Naga-inhabited areas in neighboring states of Assam, Arunachal and Manipur.

30. All India Christian Council, New Delhi
31. Council of Baptist Churches of Northeast India (CBCNEI), Guwahati
32. Council of Nagalim Churches, Kohima
33. Nagaland Missionary Movement Dimapur, Nagaland
34. United Christian Forum, Nagaland
35. Forum for Naga Reconciliation (FNR), Nagaland. FNR is openly working to unite NSCM(IM), NSCN (K) and NNC/FGN so that they can acquire bargaining strength with GOI for their sovereignty demand. Forum for Naga reconciliation organized a prayer for 'highest level meeting' of Naga political leaders (leaders of NSCN (IM), NSCN(K) and NNC (FGN) on 12 September 2010 throughout Naga inhabited areas in Nagaland and the world. FNR stated that along with Naga people, Christian communities from Australia, Denmark, Germany, Italy, UK, Singapore, Thailand, the US, Philippines, Burma, Finland, Sweden, Korea, Hong Kong, Cambodia and American Baptist Convention, African Baptist Union, European Baptist Union, Quakers Baptist Peace Fellowship of North America and the Baptist Peace Network of the Asian Baptist Federation joined the Nagas in prayer 12 September 2010.

International NGOs in nexus with NSCN (IM)[1]

1. **National Council for International Visitors** (NCIV): The NCIV provides the integral 'behind-the-scenes' national support necessary for its network of citizens' diplomats to bridge

cultures and build mutually beneficial relationship through international exchanges. The US Department of State, Office of International Visitors, is the primary partner of the National Council for International Visitors in strengthening the NCIV network's capacity.

2. **Netherlands Centre for Indigenous People, (NCIV), Amsterdam:** It is an NGO based in Amsterdam which has been supporting the promotion and protection of the rights of Indigenous People worldwide, since 1969.
3. **Grants for the Rights of Indigenous Peoples (GRIP):** GRIP financially helps NCIV for extending help to indigenous people in their initiations for the right to self-determination and decision-making.
4. **Quakers:** The Religious Society of Friends also known as Quakers is a movement that began in England in the 17th century. Today, there are approximately 600,000 Quakers in different countries of world, including India. Its stated aim is to abolish slavery, acknowledge equal rights and end warfare.
5. **Unrepresented Nations and Peoples Organization (UNPO):** It is an international non-violent and democratic membership organization. Its members are indigenous peoples, minorities and unrecognized or occupied territories who have joined together to protect and promote their human and cultural rights. UNPO provides an international forum to those nations and indigenous communities which are not recognized by United Nations (UN). Founded in 1991 at the Peace Palace in the Hague after the disintegration of USSR in fourteen smaller countries, UNPO has grown into a prominent and respected international forum.

6. **Amnesty International (AI) UK:** This is an international NGO founded in UK in 1961 which works for freedom from discrimination and promotion of human rights.
7. **Rights and Democracy:** Rights and Democracy (International Center for Human Rights and Democratic Development) is an NGO created by Canada's Parliament in 1988 to encourage and support the universal values of human rights and the promotion of democratic institutions and practices around the world. It has consultative status (category II) with the United Nations Economic and Social Council and is on the International Labour Organization's (ILO) Special List of NGOs. It also has observer status with the African Commission on Human and Peoples' Rights.
8. **Forum Asia:** It is an Asian Forum for Human Rights and Development with 40 member organizations in 15 countries in Asia. It seeks to facilitate dialogue, capacity-building and networking among human rights defenders, civil society actors and organizations in Asia to achieve full realization of all the human rights and human developments in the region. It works in league with human rights organizations.
9. **Geneva Call:** Geneva Call is an international humanitarian organization dedicated to engaging armed non-state actors (NSA) to respect and to adhere to humanitarian norms starting with the ban on anti-personnel (AP) mines.
10. **Parliamentarians for National Self-Determination (PNSD)** PNSD is a body that claims to represent "aspiring nation-states" and speaks on behalf of the Welsh, Scottish, Naga, Sikh, Kashmiri, Assamese, Manipuri, Kosovar, Kurdish and Tamil

"nations" as well as other contributors, who have welcomed the formation of this new cross party group. PNSD, a cross party group of Westminster Parliamentarians aims to highlight the importance of self-determination as a fundamental human rights as prescribed by international law as well as to promote it as a means of conflict resolution by peaceful and democratic means.

The United Nations (UN) dominated by the US, the UK and their allies played a very destructive role in fragmenting the former USSR into fourteen smaller countries and the division of Indonesia into two, giving birth to East Timor–a Christian-dominated region after its conversion from Islam to Christianity. UN had a similar role in the former Yugoslavia. PNSD in cooperation with UNPO and other such NGOs seeks to play a role in promoting the process for self determination initiated by different indigenous groups leading to independence on the lines of creation of East Timor. PSND's luminaries include several British members of parliament who are openly hostile to India and have no qualms in expressing their support for secessionist movements aimed at breaking up of our nation.

11. **Kreddha:** Kreddha–the International Peace Council for States, Peoples and Minorities–is an NGO guided by a council of eminent persons from all parts of the world dedicated to the prevention and sustainable resolution of (violent) conflicts between population groups and the government of states within which they live.
12. **Society for Threatened Peoples:** International Society for Threatened Peoples–(GfbV-International) campaigns against

all forms of genocide and ethnocide. It has sections and offices in Germany, Austria, Switzerland, Luxembourg, Italy, Bosnia-Herzegovina, Chile and Iraqi Kurdistan who work to achieve common goals as specified in its International Mission Statement.

13. **Naga International Support Centre (NISC):** NISC has been set up to focus attention on a very real but forgotten conflict that resulted, in the words of NISC, in a raging war on the frontiers of northeast Bharat and Myanmar, between the Naga peoples, Bharat and Myanmar. It says that Nagaland is inaccessible to outsiders because of India's travel restrictions. In the interest of human rights and specifically, the right to self-determination, NISC stands by the 'oppressed' Naga peoples. NISC operates from the UK and Amsterdam.
14. **International Work Group for Indigenous Affairs (IWGIA)** IWGIA's international secretariat is based in Copenhagen, Denmark. It runs a documentation centre/library and is responsible for dissemination of information, documentation and publication of books and periodicals on indigenous affairs. Its board members also include Christian Luithui, Tangkhul Naga.
15. **Indigenous Peoples' Center for Documentation, Research and Information (DOCIP):** It is a Swiss NGO established in 1978 linking Indigenous People and the United Nation. It provides support to the Indigenous Peoples' Movement for Self-determination and is funded by the European Community (European Initiatives for Democracy and Human Rights), the Swiss Agency for Development and Cooperation, the State

of Geneva, the city of Geneva and Rights and Democracy.

16. **The Voice of Martyrs, USA:** The Voice of Martyrs is a non-profit, inter-denominational organization for aiding Christians around the world being prosecuted for their faith in Christianity and spreading propaganda about the ongoing persecution of Christians.
17. **The 700 Club:** The 700 Club is the flagship news talk show of the Christian Broadcasting Network (CBN) airing on Cable's ABC family and in syndication throughout the United States and Canada. The 700 Club strongly supports Israel especially in its conflict with Palestinians and the UN. Religious issues are presented with a distinct Pentecostal flavour.
18. **USAID (US Agency for International Development):** The United State helps those people striving to live in a free and democratic country. This US foreign assistance has the two-fold purpose of furthering America's foreign policy interests, in expanding its tentacles in the name of democracy and free markets. USAID has working relationships with more than 3,500 American companies and over 300 US-based private voluntary organizations (NGOs).
19. **World Vision (WV):** World Vision International is a Christian relief and development organization working for the well-being of Christian people, especially children. Established in 1950 and working in six continents, World Vision is the largest Church-funding agency pouring money into India for secessionist forces and rapid mass-conversion.
20. **World Council of Churches:** World Council of Churches (WCC) is the broadest and most inclusive among the many

organized expressions of the inclusive modern ecumenical movement, a movement whose goal is Christian Unity. It brings together more than 340 church organizations, denominations and church fellowships in over 100 countries and territories in the globe representing some 550 million Christians. The world's largest body, the Roman Catholic Church is not a member of the WCC but works closely with the Council.

21. **Burma Lawyer's Council (BLC):** Burma Lawyers Council is an organization of lawyers which is an integral part of the pro-democracy resistance movement.
22. **Communications Co-ordination Committee for the United Nations (CCC/UN):** The Communications Co-Ordination Committee for the United Nations (CCC/UN) is to facilitate the interchange of information among civil society organizations, the United Nations and the public in order to promote more profound understanding of world problems, their effective solutions and rapid implementation.
23. **Congressional Human Rights Caucus (CHRC), USA:** Founded in 1983. The CHRC has become the leading voice in congress on human rights issues which is open to every Senator and House Member of US Congress.
24. **Asia Indigenous Peoples Pact (AIPP):** The AIPP Foundation is a regional organization conceived by indigenous people's organization in 1988 to strengthen the process of building cooperation and solidarity among indigenous peoples of Asia.
25. **The Carter Foundation (TCF):** The Carter Foundation has no connection with Former US President, Jimmy Carter and his organization. It is a non-profit organization for providing

education, advocacy training, legal aid, resource management, re-entry assistance, support, encouragement and liaison services for the prisoners, family members and community.

26. **The Carter Center:** The Carter Center, in partnership with Emory University, is committed to advancing human rights and alleviating unnecessary human suffering and was founded in 1982 by former US President Jimmy Carter and former First Lady Rosalyn Carter, and is based in Atlanta, US. Despite its "neutral" pretences, Jimmy Carter wrote to Dr Manmohan Singh, India's Prime Minister to "solve" the Naga issue by conceding to NSCN-IM demands.
27. **The International Forum on Globalization (IFG):** The IFG formed in 1994 is a North-South research and educational institution composed of leading activists, economists, scholars and researchers providing analysis and critiques on the cultural, social, political and environmental impacts of economic globalization.
28. **Indian American Center for Political Awareness (IACPA):** IACPA is an organization dedicated to serving the Indian American community in the United States.
29. **The United Nations Commission on Human Rights (UNCHR):** UNCHR comprises 53 States (Nations) meets each year in regular session in March/April for six weeks in Geneva. Over 3,000 delegates from member and observer States (Nations) and from non-governmental organizations (NGOs) participate. Its procedures and mechanisms are mandated to examine, monitor and publicly report either on human rights situations in specific countries or territories

(known as country mechanisms or mandates).

30. **KWIA (The Flemish Support Group for Indigenous Peoples):** KWIA is a support group for indigenous peoples in Belgium. It is accredited to the UNCCD.
31. **Naga American Council (NAC):** NAC is an organization which acts as a bridge between Naga rebels and their American sympathizers. It was founded in 2003 with a mission to address the Naga people's right to self-determination from India.
32. **Naga American Foundation (NAF), USA:** This is another Naga organization in the US working for Naga rebels. David Jamir–a Naga missionary from Mokokchung (Nagaland) has been working in the US, and is now an associate pastor in Baker Memorial in St. Charles.
33. **European Alliance with Indigenous People (EIPA) Brussels, Belgium:** This is a human rights group instigating Naga rebels to revolt against India.
34. **Naga Support Group, (NSG) UK:** After year of successful mission for Nagalim in South Korea and many other countries, Prof Timothy Kaping moved to Great Britain in July 2005 and founded Naga Support Group (NSG) UK in May 2006. Prof Timothy Kaping was earlier with the NSCN-IM.
35. **Naga Vigil Human Rights Group (NVHRG):** It is an international NGO founded in 1989 by David P Ward from Edinburgh, Scotland, UK supported by another British citizen Stephen Hill. Its propaganda mechanism helps NSCN (IM) get publicity in the international media.
36. **Baptist World Alliance:** Baptist World Alliance (BWA) encourages Nagaland churches in uniting various Naga militant

secessionist organizations like NSCN (IM), NSCN (K) and NNC. It stands for networking the Baptist family for conversion of the world to Christianity.

37. **NPFNK:** This is an international NGO helping NSCN (IM).
38. **Tebtebba (International Peoples' International Center for Policy Research and Education):** This is an organization that advocates the rights of indigenous peoples worldwide. Established in 1996 by Ms Victoria Tauli-Carpuz in Northern Philippine, it helps NSCN (IM) in Nagaland.
39. **United Nations Permanent Forum on Indigenous Issues (UNPFII):** This is an NGO advocating indigenous peoples' rights. Ms Victoria Tauli-Carpuz of Philippines is also the Chairman of this outfit.
40. **Cordillera Peoples' Alliance (CPA), Philippines**
41. **Global Council of Indian Christians, New Delhi.**
42. **United Nations Office on Drugs and Crime (UNODC):** This organization is aimed at strengthening the capacity of governments and civil society organizations (NGOs) in preventing drug abuse. It helps self-help group (SHG) for young women.
43. **Internet, YouTube:** This is an Internet website spreading propaganda in favour of the NSCN (IM)'s anti-national movement.

Foreign media support for NSCN (IM)[2]

1. Christian Broadcasting Network
2. Regent University
3. Trinity Broadcasting Network
4. Christian Television Network
5. Sky Angel

6. Miracle Channel
7. Daystar
8. Benny Hinn
9. Franklin Graham
10. Church Without Walls
11. Kay Arthur
12. World Magazine
13. The "Fish" Radio Network
14. National Religious Broadcasters (have a booth at their annual convention) Voice of the Martyrs
15. ABC
16. CBS
17. NBC/MSNBC
18. FOX–Kelly Wright
19. CNN
20. UPN
21. WB
22. PBS
23. Clear Channel Communication
24. Time Magazine
25. Newsweek
26. US News and World Report
27. New York Times
28. Los Angeles Times
29. New York Post
30. Chicago Tribune
31. Boston Globe
32. Atlanta Journal-Constitution

33. Denver Post
34. Kansas City Star
35. USA Today
36. Washington Arts Group (Naga Art Exhibit)
37. Sojourners Magazine
38. Foreign Affairs
39. Christianity Today Kevin Miller
40. Charisma Magazine
41. Vision Video–Ken Curtis
42. David Aikman
43. AIM International–Bill Mckay
44. Focus on the Family
45. Far East Broadcasting Company

Foreign Church Organizations helping NSCN (IM)[3]

1. The Harbor Church, Dane Justis, Associate Pastor, P O Box C, Harbor City, CA 90710, (310) 325–0373, www.theharborchurch.org
2. Del Aire Assembly of God, Pastor AI Weiss, Hawthrone, CA
3. Granada Hills Assembly of God, Pastor Dennis Schreiber, Granada Hills, CA
4. Community Christian Church, Pastor Darrell Dement, San Pedro, CA
5. Rolling Hills Covenant Church, Bob Cubillos, Rolling Hills Estates, CA (310) 521-5251
6. Every Nation Ministries, Leo Lawson, Rolling Hills Estates, CA (310) 722-1942
7. Win and Caroline Baggett, Spring Branch, TX (830) 885 5759

8. Midland Christian Fellowship (Full Gospel Evangelistic Association), Kurt Bezinque, (432) 685-1981
9. World Missions Advance, Randy Bozartb, (972) 709-9900
10. Duane and Ruth Bradley, (262) 652-6525
11. East Lake Community Church, Chula Vista, CA, Amy Branley, Assistant Children's Pastor, (619) 421-4100
12. Campus Crusade for Christ, Vonette Bright
13. John and Kerry Carmichael, Toronto, Canada, (416) 925-5457
14. Rev David Cauley, New Bern, NC, (252) 636-3032
15. Jan Dargatz, Tulsa, OK, (918) 744-6717
16. Christ For the Nations, Miralee Fosha, (214) 302-6226
17. Newport Mesa Christian Center, Costa Mesa, CA, Gabe Gaeta, Children's Pastor, (714) 966-0454
18. Bob and Debbie Mason, Missions International, (817) 410-7706
19. Elizabeth and Roger Norris, Danville, CA (925) 837-3635
20. Kerel and Darina Sedlacek, Prague, Czech Republic, Sediacekpost.
21. Paul and Cindy Shirley, (972) 492-9656
22. Harry and Elizabeth Stweart, Lexington, Kentucky, (859) 278-6755
23. Long Beach First Nazarene Church, Ron and Carole Webb, (714) 897-9305
24. Steve and Jarnie Wygant, Colorado (720) 898-0502
25. New Life' Christian Fellowship, Ponte Vedra Beach, FL, Pastor Paul and Sharon Zink, (904) 223-6000
26. Advocates International, Sam Ericsson, Fairfax, VA, (703) 764-0011

27. Christ For All Nations, Reinhard Bonnke, Orlando, FL, (407) 251-7000
28. Faith Exchange Fellowship, Pastors Dan and Ami Strattor, New York, www.faithexchange.org
29. Global Advance, David Shibley
30. Gospel for Asia, Canoilton, TX, 1-800-Win-Asia
31. Living Water International, Jeny Wiles, Houston, TX, (281) 261-7984
32. Samaritan's Purse, Franklin Graham
33. World Missionary Assistance Plan, (818) 843-7233
34. Brooklyn Tabernacle, Pastor Frank O'Neil, (718) 290-2000
35. Billy Graham–International Baptist Missionary from Britain who held several missionary crusades in Nagaland in 1972 that expedited conversion of Nagas at gunpoint and propelled Naga terrorism.

Foreign Church Leaders Helping NSCN (IM)[4]

1. Rev Dr Z Allen Abbott, Denominational Executive, West Lebanon, New Hampshire
2. Rev Carol Jamieson Brown, Pastor, First Baptist Church, Park Forest, Illinois
3. Rev Jesse M Brown, Pastor, First Baptist Church, Chicago, Illinois
4. Rev Dr Wesley H Brown, Retired Professor, Claremont California
5. Rev Dr Cheryl A Brown, Retired Professor, Claremont, California
6. Rev Ronald E Carey, Pastor, Lansing, Michigan
7. Rev John W Carlson, Retired Pastor, St Paul Minnesota

8. Rev Cedric C Cox, Retired Pastor, First Baptist Church, Indianapolis, Indiana
9. Rev Donald Crider, Retired Pastor, Huntingdon, Pennsylvania
10. Rev Herbert Dominguez. Retired Executive Minister, Bellevue Heights, Arizona
11. Rev Paul R Edie, Retired Denominational Executive, Colorado Springs, Colorado
12. Rev William Englund, Pastor, First Baptist Church St Paul, Minnesota
13. Rev Daniel Flores, Retired Executive Minister, Juncos, Puerto Rico
14. Rev Dr Louis George, Retired Executive Minister, Concord, New Hampshire
15. Rev Dr Stephen Jones, Pastor, First Baptist Church, Seattle, Washington
16. Rev Rheanolte LeBarbour, Retired Pastor, Hilton, New York
17. Rev John Laney, Pastor, Brentwood, Tennessee
18. Rev Dr Fred Lewis, Pastor, First Baptist Church, Indianapolis, Indiana
19. Rev Dawn N Mays, Retired Pastor, Westville, New Jersey
20. Rev Carol McVetty, Pastor, North Shore Baptist Church, Chicago, Illinois
21. Rev Dr William R Myers, Sr. Seminary President Emeritus, Lombard, Illinois
22. Rev John H Pipe, Pastor, Denver, Colorado
23. Rev Wayne Rogers, Retired Pastor, Dekalb, Illinois
24. Rev Ronald Schlosser, Retired Pastor, King of Prussia, Pennsylvania
25. Rev Dr James A Scott Retired Pastor, Windham, Vermont

26. Rev Ken Sehested, Pastor, Circle of Mercy Congregation, Ashville, North Carolina
27. Rev Dr Robert E Shaw, Retired Denominational Executive, Overland Park, Kansas
28. Rev Wayne Shireman, Retired Pastor, Ames, lowa
29. Rev Dr Gordon E Smith, Retired Denominational Executive, St Paul, Minnesota
30. Rev Dr Daniel E Weiss, Retired General Secretary, Naples, Florida
31. Rev Dr F Eugene Wright, Retired Pastor, Fresno, California

Foreigners under Naga Solidarity Group Supporting NSCN (IM)[5]

1. Dino Latiri, Italy
2. Thomas Labadie, France
3. Rosalinda Cameron, USA
4. Jacob Grebel, Germany
5. Thomas Johansen, Denmark
6. Julie Rickart, UK
7. Klaartje Koenig, The Netherlands
8. Marcus Betz, Germany
9. Carlotta Bellini, Italy
10. Sophia Kennell, Switzerland
11. Konard Simons, Austria
12. Elizabeth Kapu, Zimbabwe
13. Danny O'Sullivan, UK
14. Brian Cuthburt, Australia
15. Jacqueline Holmes, Canada

16. Ricardo Torres, Chile
17. Georgette Brown, USA
18. Esteban Arelleno, Mexico
19. Juan Guitterez, Columbia
20. Seiku Young, Hong Kong
21. Lena Ulrich, Germany
22. Natasha Katz, Belarus
23. David Anderson, USA
24. Michelline Formby, Rwanda
25. Connier Mahoney, UK
26. Arturo Mannet, Switzerland
27. Mustapha Sowah, Sierra Leone
28. Cynthia Oo Hong Kong
29. Katie Ehrisman, Argentina
30. Chutima Goldman, Thailand
31. Paul Dobson, South Africa

Other important foreigners working for NSCN (IM)

1. **Barbara Levy Boxer:** Barbara Levy Boxer (Jewish) is an American politician and the current Junior US Senator (Democratic Party) from the State of California.
2. **Grace Lyu Collins:** She is Tangkhul lady from Ukhrul (Manipur) who graduated from Boston College in 1985 in Fine Arts (Mixed Media and Business), MBA from the University of Durham, UK. She is associated with many NGOs, some connected with UN. She has been speaking for NSCN (IM) in churches and art museuMs Collins delivered a message from the US–"We as American Christians are praying for Naga

Christians' freedom" and brought 42 hand-sized American flags (rolled up like cigarettes) to plant in Naga areas as gifts of encouragement for the sovereignty demand of NSCN (IM). The Goodwill Mission to Nagaland on 16-27 May 2007 led by her had sent fifty-one invitations to various influential US citizens including George W Bush, the then US President, and Condoleeza Rice, then US Secretary of State, for public relations purposes.

3. **Charles Hack:** He is a journalist with a Brooklyn-based chain of weekly newspapers and lifestyle magazines. He was a member of the Goodwill Mission that visited Nagaland during 16-27 May 2005.
4. **John Houtihan:** A photojournalist from UK who visited Nagaland during 16-27 May 2005 as a member of Goodwill Mission.
5. **Sheldon Baker:** She is the founder of Harvest Projects International Inc., earned her Ph.D in Christian education and is an accomplished artist. She is also a Bible teacher and revivalist and visited Nagaland during 16-27 May 2007 as a member of Goodwill Mission.
6. **Mark Pritchett:** He is the Project Administrator for American Christian Trust, involved in equipping American Christians to help Christians of the World, and is also a member of Goodwill Mission.
7. **Leslie Richards:** A resident of Southern California, Leslie worked for 17 years as a registered nurse specializing in Oncology (Chemo and Radiation) and Aids patients. She visited Nagaland during 16-27 May 2007 as a member of Goodwill Mission.

8. **Condoleeza Rice:** Born to a Presbyterian missionary on 14 November 1954 in Birmingham, Alabama, Condoleeza Rice became the 66th Secretary of State of United States on 26 January 2005 replacing Colin Powell. She was previously George W Bush's National Security Advisor during 2001-2005. Forbes' magazine named her the world's most powerful woman in 2004 and 2005. From 1989 to March 1991, the period of German reunification and the final days of the Soviet Union, Rice served in the Bush Administration as Director and then Senior Director of Soviet and East European Affairs in the National Security Council and as Special Assistant to the President for National Security Affairs. She played a significant role in fragmenting the USSR. The same lady is now helping NSCN (IM) for balkanizing our country. Condoleeza Rice, widely regarded as a hawk, said shortly before the war in Iraq; "The United States has always reserved the right to try and diminish or eliminate the threat before it is attacked."
9. **Nazir Ahmed, Baron Ahmed:** Nazir A B Ahmed (b.1958) is Labour Member of House of Lords. In 1998, he was made Britain's second Muslim peer. Nazir Ahmed was born in the Mirpur area of Kashmir and was brought up in the UK. In 1998, Ahmed was appointed to the House of Lords and took his oath on the *Quran*.
10. **Yash Ghai:** Born in Kenya in an Indian family, Prof Ghai was trained as a lawyer at Oxford and Harvard and was called to the English Bar by the Middle Temple in London and has been a visiting professor in many countries.
11. **Victoria Tauli-Carpuz:** She is an Igorot from Philippines

working as a development consultant and indigenous activist. She has been involved in over a hundred NGOs in the US, UK and the Philippines.

12. **Jimmy and Rosalyn Carter:** Both husband and wife, the former ex-President of the US are in league with Naga terrorists under the banner of NSCN(IM).

The American Goodwill Mission to Nagaland

A Goodwill Mission team from the US visited Nagaland from 16-27 May 2005 and prepared a white paper and signed affidavits regarding 'genocide' (as the mission team preferred to call it) committed by the Government of India in the past and present on the Naga 'nation' (that is how the mission report referred to Nagaland). This report was to be registered with the Department of Justice (of the US), disseminated to US officials and finally presented to Kofi Annan, Secretary General of United Nations for further action.

The Naga Mother Association (NMA) and Naga Student Federation (NSF) hosted the mission team and these two hosts facilitated the teams' movements in and around Nagaland. In a letter enclosed with highly malicious and anti-Indian content addressed to George W Bush, then President of the US, the team members requested Bush to use his wisdom, moral conscience and international clout to influence the Government of India to (i) withdraw their over two lakh army troops from Nagaland (ii) repeal Indian Constitutional Laws (a) Armed Forces Special Power Act, 1958 (AFSPA, 1958) and (b) Restricted Area Permit (RAP) because of which more than three lakh lives were lost.

They requested Bush to denounce India as Christians suffered at the hands of Hindu "extremists". Bush was requested to extend financial assistance directly to the "Naga government" (Govt. of People's Republic of Nagalim (GPRN) of NSCN-IM) since they have many natural resources to offer (to the US) such as vast oil reserves, uranium and gold. It is stated in the letter that Naga people loyally fought side by side with America and allied forces in both World Wars, now it was time for those allied forces to support the Nagas. (Nagas under the leadership of A Z Phizo fought side-by-side Indian National Army-INA led by Subhash Chandra Bose against allied forces led by the US and the UK).

It will not be out of context to recall how the US/UK combine waged war, under the pretext of liberating Kuwait, to overthrow Saddam Hussein of Iraq in order to plunder crude oil and other minerals from those countries. The Western allies also balkanized the USSR into fourteen smaller countries, separated East Timor (now a Christian-dominated country) from Indonesia (a Muslim country but with Indian cultural heritage) and are still helping Pakistan and Bangladesh to foment terrorism in India's Jammu & Kashmir and Northeast region besides other parts of our country. The Mission's letter to Bush appealed that the US and the United Nations should take a closer look at Naga peace talks, monitoring the ceasefire Agreement between National Socialist Council of Nagalim–Isak-Muivah (NSCN-IM) and GOI, creating a US presence in Nagalim and assisting the Nagas' desire for "full-fledged independence". The letter complains that the India government has not offered any solution even after 60 rounds of talks. It demands international intervention to fulfill their demand of interdependent co-federal relationship. This "interdependent co-federal relationship" is the latest coinage of the NSCN-IM to camouflage its demand for sovereignty.

The Role of the Church

In 1872, American missionaries entered Nagaland and forced Nagas to convert to Christianity. The Angamis of Khonoma, Mezoma and Kekrima revolted against British Rule and Christian conversion. Haipou Jadonang, Rani Gaidinlui of Manipur and the Chakhesangs of Thevopisumi village too revolted against them. The saying goes on–the Bible follows the bullet, Nagas were converted at gunpoint. After 1947, Naga National Council (NNC) under the Chairmanship of Phizo formed a nexus with American Baptist Missionaries. Michael Scott, a British missionary was friend, philosopher and guide of Phizo and NNC. He was later expelled from the country by Nehru. The Church psychologically weaned away Nagas from Indian society and incited them to wage a war of independence against India. They distorted the history of Nagas and compiled concocted stories to keep Nagas away from the national mainstream. This is a war that still continues.

In the case of Nagas, the Church has been quite successful in its conspiracy of severing the joint at the 30 kilometers wide Siliguri corridor from the rest of the country. The Naga insurgency has come a long way and the enlightened section of Naga society realizes today the futility of militancy by misguided sections of Naga society. Naga militants are fragmented into several groups, but the Church acts as their godfather. The NSCN (IM), led by Isak Chishi Swu, Chairman and Th Muivah, General Secretary is comparatively a stronger militant group. Local and international church and non-governmental organizations are now very close to NSCN-IM and they are helping it in all respects. With a view to internationalize the domestic problem pertaining to Naga society, this American Goodwill Mission toured Nagaland from 16-27 May 2007 and tried their level best to establish Christian solidarity with US Christians. The Nagaland Church has also come forward in establishing this solidarity by declaring the state as "Nagaland for Christ" where only Christianity is the recognized religion. Conversions to Christianity and Naga insurgency go hand-in-hand, with the Church and militant organizations helping each other. NSCN-IM has reportedly nearly 3,500 trained militants.

America has a reason to help NSCN-IM

There is no Christian country in the Third World. Right from Israel up to Japan, including countries like Iran, Iraq, Afghanistan, Pakistan, China, Bangladesh, Bharat and other smaller countries, there is no Christian country in an area where 375 crore people live, something that worries the nexus of the US, UK, and the Vatican. They want to create a Christian country and Greater Nagaland which NSCN-IM now refers to as Nagalim, if carved out, would be the first proposed Christian country in the subcontinent. This strategy of America is an echo of the late Pope John Paul II's declaration, "Europe was won over in first millennium, Africa and America in second millennium. Now in third millennium Asia must be won over." In Asia, Communist and Muslim countries have banned the preaching of Christianity. The only reason Bharat is a prime target is because of Hindu tolerance. The

Church's means are Bible (forced conversion), booze (destruction of youths by preaching the philosophy of hedonic consumerism, addiction to liquor and sexual promiscuity) and bullet (NSCN-IM resorts to violence in Arunachal, Manipur and Nagaland for forced conversion). Because of its strategic location, Northeast Bharat prominently figures in the map of conversion plan of the US/UK combine and Vatican/Pope's mercenaries. The US Senate has constituted the Senate Foreign Relations Committee on Nagaland. Almost all preceding US Consul Generals posted at Kolkata have paid visits to Nagaland. On some occasions, their visits have been disallowed because of their mala fide intensions, clandestine activities and hobnobbing with the Church and secessionist Naga guerillas.

I have ventured to run an investigation into the US government's disturbing support to evangelical organizations engaged in Church-planting, intelligence gathering and conversions across the country. Simultaneously, I ran an investigation into native and foreign NGOs dubious role to disintegrate Bharat with special reference to Nagaland and NSCN(IM). These NGOs and Church organizations are supported by America's Central Intelligence Agency (CIA) and Pakistan's Inter-Services Intelligence (ISI). The erstwhile Bush administration encouraged Christian faith-based organizations like no other administration did before. Their conversion campaign runs worldwide, but Bharat is a major laboratory. They use everything from classical conversion techniques to state-of-the-art technology in their efforts.

Over the past decades, American, British, Australian and other foreign missionaries have repeatedly violated Bharat's laws banning their entry, by coming in on tourist visas and indulging in conversion and Church-planting in Nagaland. These churches are the bases of NSCN(IM) and other Naga terrorists. Naga missionaries and Church activists are zealous evangelists and harbingers of the Naga secessionist movement, prodded on by their American and British masters. Now, Christianity has become a corporate or political campaign for Naga politicians like Neiphiu Rio-former Chief Minister of Nagaland and his political partner-BJP (Nagaland).

There is another, more important reason why Bush was keen on supporting his evangelist friends who run huge Transnational Missionary Organizations (TMOs). In the decade 1990-2000, they ran a global intelligence operation so complex and sophisticated that its scale and implications are staggering. These missionary-run intelligence operations have put in place a system which enables the US government to access any ethnographic information on any location virtually, at the click of the mouse. This network in Bharat, established with funding and strategic assistance from US-based TMOs, gives US intelligence agencies virtually real-time access to every nook and corner of the country.

Multi-billion enterprises run by evangelists like Pat Robertson, Billy Graham and Roger Houtsma, amongst many others, were instrumental in running a coordinated conversion campaign in Bharat under the banner of AD 2000, which later became a Joshua Project. Joshua Project II was launched to sustain the time-bound conversions and intelligence gathering and was planned on a military model with the intent to invade, occupy, control and subjugate its population. The idea was to foment communal uprising in Hindu society in the name of Dalit rights, untouchability, ethnicity, caste, creed, language and class. The movement that took shape over the 1990s, has now taken off because of a unique collaboration between American government and US-based evangelical mission agencies. This movement was also a massive intelligence gathering exercise, funded and supported by American missionary organizations, that were responsible for the election of George W Bush. North and Northeast region of Bharat were strategically important for the missionaries.

The new buoyancy in Indo-US relations has made things easier. Tremendous energy has been spent on "spying out" the land and its inhabitants. This American mission involves thousands of Church pastors, reverends, evangelists, laity, priests and clergymen on the pay-roll of the CIA, posted in the churches of Nagaland and NE states and other strategic places of North Bharat. They are handsomely paid for supplying classified information with regard to military-bases, army-movements, defence strategies, maps of strategic places, roads linking international borders, defence factories, thermal power stations, fuel installations, Science Research Centers etc. The collaboration between American missionaries now replaced by Naga missionaries, CIA and NSCN(IM) is working on creating a Christian country–Nagalim which will be a base for America and Britain.[6]

Ceasefire opposed

Prior to the ceasefire agreement on 1 August 1997 with GOI under the then Prime Minister H D Deve Gowda and NSCN-IM, the latter was breathing its last. Th Muivah was openly advertising in local media for recruitment to his armed cadre. When there was no response from Naga youths, NSCN-IM offered rupees five lakh in addition to a monthly salary. Even after that, the insurgents could not get any response from the Naga youths. But H D Deve Gowda succumbed to international pressure and entered into the ceasefire agreement on 1August 1997, thus providing a lease of life to NSCN-IM. They collected crores of rupees through extortion and from international NGOs through hawala and other illegal means. NSCN-IM guerrillas strutted about on the roads while Indian soldiers were confined to barracks.

Dr S C Jamir, who was the Chief Minister of Nagaland, was not consulted about the ceasefire agreement and therefore opposed it. The army was also opposed to this agreement. What made GOI to enter such a dubious agreement is still a mystery. Dr S C Jamir's staunch opposition to the sovereignty demand of NSCN-IM provoked Muivah who tried to kill him, with almost half a dozen assassination attempts on the chief minister's life. In 1993, Jamir was brutally attacked by NSCN-IM militants in Nagaland House, New Delhi. His body was riddled with bullets but luckily, the doctors of All India Institute of Medical Services saved his life. In 1995, NSCN-IM guerillas in Kohima sprayed AK-47 bullets, from close range, at Jamir's car when he was returning home after visiting his daughter's place. The impact of the bullets threw the car 30 metres down the steep slope until it dashed against a pine tree and stopped. Inside, Jamir and his wife were found a live with minor injuries. In 1999 in between Piphema and Medziphema, fourteen powerful bombs were detonated simultaneously, followed by a hail of AK 47 bullets from three sides when Jamir's convoy was passing through a narrow stretch of NH-39, the extreme by steep terrain. The bombs missed the Jamir's car and he was safe. But a hail of bullets from sophisticated weapons killed two security personnel on the spot and wounded several more. Jamir escaped miraculously.

It was indeed unfortunate that even the Vajpayee Government remained silent over this incident. In 2007 November, the NSCN-IM declared Jamir, Governor of Goa, 'anti-national', 'anti-Naga', 'traitor' and so on. It ordered him not to enter into Nagaland or else 'face the consequences'. The Democratic Alliance of Nagaland (DAN) Government led by Neiphiu Rio and joined by Bharatiya Janata Party (BJP) as the coalition partner remained shockingly silent. The reason for their silence was that they had captured political power in 2003 state elections when NSCN-IM had hijacked the election and ordered voters at gunpoint to vote only for DAN candidates. How could a separatist organization ban the entry of the Governor of an Indian state into Nagaland? The stunning silence of the union government was equally shocking. On 24 November 2007, Goa Governor was ambushed at Changki village in Mokokchung district of Nagaland while he was retuning to Dimapur after visiting his home district. Five IED's exploded on the spot of ambush followed by a rain of AK bullets from two sides to ensure the sure death of Governor Jamir. Two-inch mortars thrown at the Governor's vehicle miraculously failed to explode. Besides, the police found other improvised explosive devices (IEDs) which could not be triggered off. Governor Jamir again escaped unhurt. NSCN-IM became frustrated over its failure to assassinate Jamir this time too. When spontaneous condemnation of NSCN-IM poured in from several NGOs, civil organizations and the public, NSCN-IM's escuse was that it was "stage-managed" to gain cheap popularity and public sympathy. The Neiphiu Rio-led DAN Government (the conglomeration of Naga People's Front–NPF and BJP) brushed it off as a "minor matter" under the "political problem" category. The UPA regime under Manmohan Singh has also proved to equally weak and meek in tackling the heinous deeds of NSCN-IM. Such complacence of Delhi naturally discourages patriotic Nagas who keep Kohima attached to Delhi at the risk of their lives and families. NSCN (IM) Eulogizes Neiphiu Rio as the best Chief Minister.

The American Goodwill Mission of 2005 too termed Neiphiu Rio as the best Chief Minister Nagaland has ever had and condemned Jamir as the 'Indian puppet'. This is the same Neiphiu Rio who gave a free hand to NSCN-IM and resolved to pay Rs 60 lakh each financial year to the Church for its 'developmental work'. He is the same chief minister who took up the 'plight'' of Christians throughout the country at the Chief Ministers Conference chaired by Prime Minister Manmohan Singh and asked the Prime Minister to punish Hindutvavadi 'fanatics'. Rio also asked the union government to prevail upon Myanmar to stop army operations against Christian missionaries and Naga militants.

In our country, human rights activists and communists are two segments that are virulently anti-Hindu and anti-national. They operate in a camouflaged garb so that their criminal and anti-national activities are not detected. These human rights activists and communists reward each and every individual and NGO who serves them sincerely. This is the reason for Neiphiu Rio being rewarded the "National Human Rights and Duties Award 2007" by the Indian Institute of Human Rights, New Delhi on 11 December 2007 on the occasion of 9th world Human Rights Congress and Human Rights Day at the India International Centre, New Delhi. All underground organizations, their above-ground wings working in the garb of youth organizations, tribal organizations, NGOs, human rights organizations and church bodies incessantly agitate for scrapping the Armed Forces Special Power Act 1958 and Restricted Area Permits because both the Acts restrict their anti-Indian activities and conversion crusades. Neiphiu Rio, not surprisingly, is the severest critic of these two Acts. Neiphiu Rio acts as the counselor of NSCN-IM and international church bodies with the help of BJP leaders too, in the state and Delhi. He has been quite successful in his nefarious game plan. More than 20 thousand Christians in over 100 churches in the Churachandpur district and elsewhere in the northeastern state of Manipur, launched a prayer campaign for freedom and democracy in Myanmar on 21 October 2007, expressing solidarity with political prisoners and the democratic leader Aung San Suu Kyi, who is a Christian convert. Suu Kyi's husband is another devout British Christian. The campaign was organized by Myanmar Christian Fellowship (MCF) comprising Burmese Christians in exile in collaboration with Nagaland and Manipur church organizations and Human Rights Alert of Manipur. In the name of Christian solidarity, the Myanmar Church is trying to establish close relation with the US, UK and other Christian countries. Neiphiu Rio never looses any such opportunity to show his Christian solidarity and this time too, he wrote a long letter to our Prime Minister Dr Monmohan Singh to pressurize the Myanmar government not to "disturb"

Naga undergrounds, who are helping Aung San Suu Kyi in the name of Christian solidarity.

NSCN (IM) Influence on Indian Politicians

A meeting with the leaders of the Opposition and NSCN(IM) was held at the residence of former Prime Minister V P Singh, attended by Ram Vilas Paswan, Ram Jethmalani, Left politicians D Raja, A B Bardhan, Sitaram Yechuri, Raghuvansh Prasad Singh of the RJD, human rights activist Swami Agnivesh and Abdul Rashid Saheen of National Conference. The three former prime ministers of Bharat–V P Singh, Chandra Shekhar and H D Deve Gowda–issued a statement appealing to the authorities concerned to do the needful for the release of Th Muivah who was then undergoing a jail term in Bangkok, Thailand from 19 January 2000 for travelling on a fake visa. This meeting was held in July 2000.[7]

Beware of Pseudo–Gandhians and Human Rightists

NSCN(IM) is clever enough to knock at every door to fulfil its anti-Indian demands. Muivah, though imprisoned in a Thailand jail for travelling on fake visa, managed to organize a meeting of bipartisan participants from Thailand, Bharat and various international groups on 23 July 2000 in Bangkok to "discuss" the NSCN-IM's demands. The symposium resolved (i) to appeal to Thai and Indian governments to recognize Muivah as an essential participant in the Indo-NSCN (IM) negotiations and therefore (ii) both the governments should do the needful to release Muivah from a Thai jail in Bangkok. On behalf of the 25 participants of this symposium, the above resolution was submitted to the Thai and Indian governments. The then Home Minister L K Advani got Muivah released from Bangkok jail after four months imprisonment.

Nagalim for Christ

Nagaland Baptist Council of Churches (NBCC) declared 'Nagaland for Christ' which means that only Baptist Christianity is the recognized religion in Nagaland. In 2000, NBCC declared that 10,000 Naga missionaries were being trained to take the gospel to Bharat, Nepal, Bhutan and Myanmar. NSCN (IM) echoed this declaration of NBCC. Isak Chishi Swu, Chairman of NSCN (IM) revealed in an interview at Beverly Hills (USA) that Nagaland had 10,000 missionaries poised to take the gospel to nearby lands. "We want to penetrate China, Cambodia, Burma, Vietnam, Laos, Nepal and Bhutan with the gospel" he said, "and we have 10,000 Naga missionaries who are ready to go." He said that American Baptists gave American missionaries for our Naga people and 95 per cent of Naga population has been converted (Eastern Mirror 29 August 2005). NSCN (IM)'s letter pad is marked 'Nagalim for Christ' (Nagalim means Greater Nagaland). S K Arshing, self-styled Secretary, Ministry of Religious Affairs GPRN (NSCN-IM) stated, "The strong faith and hope of the GPRN (NSCN-IM) is in Christ alone and the faith and hope GPRN (Government of People's Republic of Nagalim–NSCN-IM) has been proclaiming, witnessing and mobilizing everywhere throughout the Naga inhabited areas even outside Nagaland and abroad that we the Nagas are for Christ."

Nagas of Nagaland Reject NSCN-IM

Th Muivah and his Tangkhul cohorts have killed thousands of non-Tankhul leaders-underground and above-ground both from his Naga National Council (NCC) days onwards. The genocide of non-Tangkhul Nagas reached its peak in 1980 when Muivah and his lieutenants returned after armed training in China and after becoming "born-again" in Chinese Communism. He defected from the Church-sired NNC and formed the National Socialist Council of Nagaland (NSCN) under deep influence of Chinese communism. NSCN then reportedly destroyed 300 churches (Baptists) and killed hundreds of church leaders, pastors and reverends throughout Nagaland mostly in Mon and Tuensang districts of Nagaland and bordering Naga inhabited areas of Myanmar. Due to the Tangkhul favouritism of Muivah, a large section of non-Tangkhul Nagas, viz, Angamis, Aos, Semas, Konyaks, Chakhesangs, Lothas and Hemi Nagas from Myanmar were under anxiety. They defected from NSCN and formed NSCN (K) under the leadership of S S Khaplang–a Hemi Naga from Myanmar in 1988. Tangkhuls remained in the parent body while most of the non-Tangkhuls came to Khaplang fold within nine years. The NSCN (IM)'s camp was deserted and many cadres surrendered to the Government and yet others defected to NSCN (K) and by 1997 NSCN (IM) was breathing its last. It had lost its ground in Nagaland. It had no bargaining capacity. If the government of Bharat had continued the then existing policy of the Nagaland government under S C Jamir of exterminating the Naga terrorism led by NSCN (IM), the situation in Nagaland, Manipur, Assam and Arunachal Pradesh would have been different, to the advantage of the nation's sovereignty and strategic interests. But it is a mystery that instead of crushing the insurgency, HD Dewe Gowda government entered into a ceasefire agreement with them. This gave a new lease of life to NSCN (IM). Muivah made full use of the ceasefire agreement as a period for building up his strength because the Indian army had returned to its barracks and NSCN (IM) insurgents were now free. Muivah also used the ceasefire period to try to assassinate S C Jamir and all others who opposed the genocide led by Muivah and his Tangkhul cadres and also all those who stood for the unity, integrity and sovereignty of Bharat. Up to 2005, it ran a parallel government in Nagaland and killed over a thousand Nagas and attacked many more, including S C Jamir.

Today, NSCN(IM) has come a full circle and has reached the starting point from where it began on 1 August 1997. The strength it gathered from 1997 to 2005 has diminished and all the non-Tangkhul cadres have deserted the Hebron Camp–the Headquarter of the NSCN-IM, 30 kilometers from Dimapur. On 22 April 2007, the Wungrum village known as NSCN(IM) village near Dimapur was attacked by 5,000 strong Naga mob. Twenty houses of NSCN (IM) Kilonsers (self-styled "ministers") were burnt to ashes. A huge cache of lethal weapons was recovered without a single bullet being fired. NSCN (IM) leaders and cadres ran away from the village to escape the fury of the Nagas. Because of rampant extortion at gunpoint, wanton killings of innocent people without rhyme or reason, repeated brutal attacks on S C Jamir by Muivah's cadres, the towns, cities and villages of Nagaland are taking utmost care not to allow Muivah's cadres to enter their vicinity. Several NSCN (IM) cadres have been thoroughly thrashed and even lynched to death by the public. The Dimasa Hindus–the worst sufferers because of Hebron headquarter of Muivah's NSCN-IM, have been demanding the removal of Hebron camp. Now, other Nagas have also joined the Dimasas in their demand for removal of Hebron camp from their area. Naga parents now no longer allow their grown-up children to join NSCN(IM).

Seeing the situation adverse to NSCN(IM), Isak Chishi Swu has secretly sneaked out of the international border at Meghalaya and reached Thailand's capital Bangkok. Muivah under Z-category security is almost a prisoner in his Hebron Camp licking the dust. He is himself witnessing how Naga society has changed and Nagas are happy to remain in Bharat. Seeing his game plan fizzled out, Muivah is now spending sleepless nights in his Hebron camp. He is also looking for an opportunity to sneak out secretly to a foreign country to escape the wrath of the Naga people. Muivah had been cunning enough to coin different catchy slogans at different points of time to mesmerize Nagas. In the year 2000, he coined the word "reconciliation" to bring all factions, politicians, NGOs and church organizations into his fold. In 2007, he coined the slogan "unification" and several gimmicks were pushed. Several "unification" meetings were held at the Hebron camp, but this time it has all backfired. In the name of unification, all the Sema cadres along with all other non-Tangkhul militants have defected from NSCN-IM. They have deserted the Hebron camp and joined NSCN(K), while poor Miuvah is watching this drama unfold in a manner he might never have dreamt of.

Why the Disillusionment

A report in a Guwahati-based media outlet, also carried in Nagaland revealed that Muivah had amassed wealth worth more than Rs 300 crore and had purchased shares in different multi-national companies. The Nagas of Nagaland blame Muivah. They say that Nagaland is not the Gaza strip for rehabilitating certain Nagas from outside Nagaland (meaning Tangkhuls of Manipur). In the name of Naga nationalism, lakhs of acres of land have been occupied at gunpoint and palatial buildings established all over Nagaland. Dimapur, particularly, has been transformed into a fortress and a safe haven for Muivah's bloodsucking goons for running smuggling of guns marijuana, heroin, vehicle theft, kidnapping, extortion, killings, rape and all other kinds of anti-social activities. "Go home! Muivah and brothers! There is no space for you over here! You can no more keep the Nagas at ransom. Your principle and ideology can no longer take the Nagas for a ride. We do not need your Amsterdam, UN, UNPO, Americas etc but only peace. Leave us alone please or face the consequences. Dear Tangkhul brothers, how long do you think your tribe should be at the mercy of Muivah's arrogance, hypocrisy and obstinacy? Isn't it the right time for your community to speak up and rein in Muivah and his separatist ideology for the sake of the Nagas? Isn't there any sane and bold Tangkhul intellectual or responsible leader to resist the destruction of the tribe and the Nagas merely at the whims of corrupted and egoistic leader in the form of Muivah?"[8]

S C Jamir, who also authored *Bedrock of Naga Society*, is reported to be the man behind clipping the wings of Muivah and his Tangkhul lieutenants. It was the most anti-national act of some

Delhi politicians to target a patriot like S C Jamir who is totally committed to protecting the sovereignty of Bharat.

Central Government's Apathy

It is the duty of MHA to enquire properly into (i) the aims, objects, area of operation, modus operandi, mode of raising funds, (ii) proper utilization of funds (iii) the activity report in the light of work done on the ground and (iii) their involvement in anti-social and anti national activities (iv) bank account (v) proper maintenance of statement of income and expenditure (iv) nexus of politicians, bureaucrats, MNCs, mafia dons and terrorist organizations and (d) complacent beneficiary groups, the proper monitoring of activities, the necessary checks and adequate enquiries are not done at every level. As a result, running an NGO at national and international level has become a flourishing business.

When the government fails (i) to maintain effective ground level contact with the people and (ii) to fulfill their wishes, it becomes weakened and non-government actors become powerful. Today, it is these actors who are controlling the parallel economy in the form of black money. Foreign NGOs are successful in patronizing terrorist organizations like NSCN (IM) challenging the sovereignty of the nation. Should the government of Bharat not act decisively to check the anti-national activities of these NGOs who are helping NSCN (IM) and other terrorist organizations of their choice operating in NE region? Should GOI not be pro-active to finish Naga insurgency once for all? During every ceasefire agreement the insurgents have violated the agreement once their rebuilding work was over. Each time, they killed scores of army jawans and innocent people. This time, the Government of India should not be caught unawares. The army should be empowered to tighten the noose. The Armed Forces Special Power Act 1958 (AFSPA) should remain in force; rather, it should be made more stringent. The government of Bharat must not succumb to international pressure, pushed through their Indian stooges present in our parliament, judiciary, bureaucracy and the fourth estate–the media. The masked NGOs (national and international) and "human-rightists", mostly advocates/lawyers, retired judges and persons from socialist/communist background are required to be kept under strict surveillance and their international connections and affiliations probed. Anybody found guilty of betraying the nation and committing crimes against the society and country should be awarded exemplary punishment because crime unpunished only breeds and emboldens criminals.

The Responsibility of Civil Society

Drawing a lesson from the blatant Christian appeasement policy of the Central Government, in the grip of Sonia Gandhi who is a foreigner, a rabid Christian fundamentalist and rank Hindu-baiter, Bharatiya civil society must exercise close vigil and monitor mechanism for the on-going peace-process between NSCN(IM) and the government of India so that this time, the government is prevented from committing gross national betrayal by agreeing to anti-national demands of Naga terrorists who are in league with Naga politicians and bureaucrats.

References

1. Internet
2. *American Goodwill Mission,* 16-27 May 2005
3. *Idib*
4. *The Morung Express,* 23/03/2007
5. *Nagaland Post,* 27/03/2007
6. *Tehalka,* 07/02/2004
7. *Idib*, Internet
8. *Nagaland Post,* 11 January 2008

Uniform Civil Code: Vote-bank vs National Interest

— Meenakashi Lekhi

Article 44, earlier labelled as Article 35 in the draft file, directing that "The state shall endeavour to secure for the citizens a uniform civil code throughout the territory of India" was enacted in 1949.

What was the need to bring about this Article? as even in 1949 and to date, almost every aspect of legal relationship such as laws of contract, transfer of property, sale of goods, partnership, arbitration and limitation, crimes and criminal procedure were governed by common/uniform laws? The exception, however, was and continues to be, the laws governing marriage and succession. Thus, the need to enact Article 44 of the Constitution was the avowed intention to bring about the much-needed change and parity in personal relationships.

Personal laws may be defined as that body of laws, which apply to a person or to a matter, solely on the ground of his belonging to or being associated with a particular religion. In Mitar Sen vs Maqbul Hasson AIR 1930 pc 251(252) the Privy Council used the expressions "personal law 'and' law of religion" interchangeably, thus making the legal terminology "personal law" a very familiar expression, an expression not difficult to understand but not easy to define.

Thus, Article 44 appears to be a determined expression of the conviction of the framers of the Constitution. Different religion-based laws were and are not in tune with the egalitarian and secular philosophy of our national charter or the Constitution.

Repeatedly, the Supreme Court observed that the non-implementation of the provisions of Article 44 amounts to grave failure of Indian democracy and the sooner we take action, the better it will be. Chief Justice Gajendra Gadkar made this observation in *Secularism and the Constitution of India, 1971*. Justice Hegde in *Islamic law in Modern India, 1972*, also observed that religion-oriented personal laws were a concept of the medieval times alien to modern societies, which are secular and cosmopolitan. He further emphasized that as long as our laws are religion-oriented, we can hardly build a homogenous nation.

A five-judge bench of the Supreme Court in Shah Bano Begum's case, AIR 1985 sc 945(954), about which much ado full of sound and fury was made by fundamentalist quarters, declared unanimously in the words of Chief Justice Chandrachud, as hereunder:

> "It is also a matter of regret that Article 44 has remained a dead letter—there is no evidence of any official activity for framing a common code for the country—a common civil code will help the course of national integration by removing disparate loyalties to laws which have

> conflicting ideologies. It is the state which is charged with the duty of securing a uniform civil code for its citizens and, unquestionably, it has the legislative competence to do so. We understand the difficulties involved in bringing persons of different faiths and persuasions on a common platform. But a beginning has to be made if the constitution is to have any meaning. Inevitably, the role of reformer has to be assumed by the courts because it is so beyond the endurance of any sensitive minds to allow injustice to be suffered when it is so palpable."

In the Bai Tahira AIR 1979 SC 362, Fazlunbi AIR 1980 SC 362, before Shah Bano Begum and Jordon Diengleh vs S S Chopra, AIR 1985 SC 935 cases, the Supreme Court has expressed the immediate and compulsive need for a uniform civil code. The apex court has repeatedly expressed regret that the demand for a uniform civil code under Article 44 could generate militant activity, though in a backward direction, so much so that Muslim women, after divorce, have virtually been excluded from the operation of the uniform general law, as contained in Chapter 9 of the Code of Criminal Procedure by Muslim women (Protection of Rights on Divorce) Act, 1986, unless in a given case, both the woman and her former husband agree in writing before the magistrate, to be governed by the provision of the code.

So much for legal ingenuity. Apart from Article 44, the Supreme Court also has the powers under Article 142 which allows for the apex court to pass any order, provided such order is "necessary for doing complete justice in any case or matter pending before it." Another argument as raised by Justice Mathew in the well-known decision in Kesavananda Bharti, AIR 1973 SC 1461, held that judiciary is also "State". If the judiciary as one organ of the state, finds other organs in slumber, it can choose to awaken them from torpid stupor and make them alive to their mandatory and fundamental duty under the constitution. We must hail such a gesture.

The later judgments of the Supreme Court and other high courts have clarified that during subsistence of the first marriage, a spouse cannot change religion and remarry. He will be liable u/s 494 of the IPC. As late as March 2010, in a Delhi High Court judgment, maintenance provisions under the Criminal Procedure Code Sections 125 to 126, have been applied to grant relief to a divorced woman and her child. The courts have repeatedly held the view that reasonable and fair provision include provision for the future of the divorced wife (including maintenance) and it does not confine itself to the strict application of personal laws.

Communal divides, vote-bank politics and staunch fundamentalism are currently barriers to the realization of a uniform civil code, but with time and tolerance they can be overcome. What is perceived, as a matter of defining individual rights, has deteriorated into majority vs minority issue.

It is pertinent to mention here that while debating the draft, the sub-committee on fundamental rights, recommended that while a uniform civil code for all citizens was highly desirable, its application should be made on an entirely voluntary basis. Interestingly, this recommendation was met with dissent in clear and ringing words. A dissent note was signed by Shree Minu Masani, a Parsi, Raj Kumari Amrit Kaur, a Christian and Hansa Mehta, a Hindu. The dissent note stated that "one of the factors that has kept India back from advancing to nationhood has been the existence of the personal laws based on religion, which has kept the nation divided into watertight compartments in many aspects of life. We are of the view that a uniform civil code should be guaranteed to the Indian people within a period of five to ten years. "The advisory committee might transfer the clause regarding a uniform civil code from Part two to Part one after making suitable modifications in it."

On the other hand, Shri Mahboob Ali Baig wanted a categorical provision that "Nothing in this article shall affect the personal laws of a citizen or a community of people shall not be obliged to give its own personal law."

The argument against a uniform civil code was that this provision would run contrary to the Article 19 which guaranteed freedom of religion. A valid answer to this argument would be that Article 19 permits legislation covering secular activities. Religion is a matter of faith and spiritual character. I quote Prof Fyzee while exploring the difference between law and religion:

> "Laws are impersonal and objective rules which the state applies to all its citizens without exception. But religion is based on the personal experience of great teachers; its appeal is personal, immediate and intuitive. While the rules, their rituals and trappings can be of general application in a community, the inner core of belief is exclusively personal."

Thus, it is emphasized that there is a clear difference between the rule of law, which can be enforced by the state and rule of conscience of the minorities. The greatest difficulty in Islam is that Sharia embraces both law and religion. Religion is based on spiritual experience but law is based upon the will of the community as expressed by the legislature (in a democratic society) or any other lawmaking authority in other societies. While religion is unchangeable in its kernel, laws differ from time to time and place to place. The laws, by their very nature, must seek to change with the changing social tides. One can say that Sharia encapsulates both, the religion which is unchangeable, as also the law which is changeable. To take the argument back to the apparent contradiction between Articles 44 and 19; the answer lies in harmonions construction of the two constitutional provisions. Article 44 deals with the mundane issues of daily life and acts in a sphere which relates to the issues of marriage and succession; whereas Article 19 deals with one's relationship with God. But the issues of polygamy, triple *talaq* and maintenance cause tremendous hardships to women and hence need to be addressed and remedied by the laws. The spheres of influence being different, there is thus, no contradiction between Articles 44 and 19 of the Constitution.

This brings us to the next question, that most personal laws affect the status of the women adversely. Hence, the non-enforcement of a uniform civil code violates the rights of women. Rights which are extremely basic in nature are thus called human rights. Women's rights are also human rights and violation of these is also the violation of Articles 12, 14, 16 and 21. Article 21 specifically deals with the right to life and liberty. The right to live with dignity is compromised and it is the worst form of violation if a woman is left remediless due to polygamy, triple *talaq* or non-maintenance. I can safely argue that marriage, divorce, inheritance and other aspects of personal status are social and secular activities around religion. These being secular activities, they can very well be regulated by the state. All personal laws must be purged of all unsatisfactory elements. The conflict, if any, is assumed between Articles 44 and 19. This is further supported by the fact that Articles 25 and 26 of the constitution recognize the Indian citizen as its basic constituent unit rather than a community or a collective group defined by language, caste or religion. It is the individual citizen who has fundamental rights.

The male attitude, especially that of orthodox men gives rise to deep concern. There is deep concern for Muslim women whose rights are violated. These women approach the court for the redress of their rights. What are the courts supposed to tell such women? Should these courts send these suffering women back to the maulvis and the ulema (the Muslim clergy) or adjudicate upon these cases according to the principles of justice, equality and secularism? To come to the aid of aggrieved women, the courts must invoke the constitutional mandate and protect their individual or fundamental rights. The non-implementation of a uniform civil code is basically a case of gender injustice being inflicted upon the individual women, whose veil cannot hide the sadness of their faces and is not capable of wiping off the tears trickling from their eyes.

The reasons mostly given for non-implementation of a uniform code is that since no injustice takes place in the "pure" state of Islam, there is no requirement of addressing these issues. These people had attacked the Shah Bano judgment on the ground of it abusing real Islamic society. It is unfortunate that these people are not able to think of reform but only of a "pure" Islamic state.

Another argument being advocated against a uniform civil code is that it arouses the fear of Islam's cultural identity being in danger. My answer to this issue is twofold—one that smaller minorities do not suffer from similar insecurity and secondly, identity itself is a multi layered, complex and complicated issue. It is derived from language, food, clothes, climate and geography. On the other hand, communities are not monolithic entities and each is riddled with sects and variations of the personal law itself. Howsoever ardently one may wish, the correlation that exists in the Muslim mind between insecurity and a uniform civil code cannot be wished away. The government has failed to conduct a low-key but sustained campaign for MTP, PNDT etc for explaining the nature and advantages of the uniform civil code. This has hardened apprehensions into strong fears. The Directive Principles, which direct the state to work towards a particular goal, put a heavier burden on the executive organ of the state along with the legislature. The government has done nothing to discharge its burden; the significance of the contents of Article 44, need to be explained to the masses. This is a beneficial provision and its utility must be advocated to fight the obscurantists who oppose a uniform civil code. The undue weight given to the views of conservative sections rather than giving importance to the progressive and liberal members of the community, is another contributing factor.

The Congress-led UPA and the various Congress state governments themselves, have been reassuring the Muslims that government had/has no intention of enforcing a uniform civil code ever since 1938. Unfortunately, even when other parties have come to power in the centre, they have failed to enforce the uniform civil code. This observation is especially relevant when the state of Goa follows the Portuguese code, at par with a uniform civil code and other states have chosen to remain quiet on this issue. In spite of law and order being a state subject and the Supreme Court having given its mandate repeatedly on this issue, one can see through the vote-bank politics being employed by various stakeholders.

The role played by minority politicians is far from constructive. Their attitude is to feed the Muslim mind with fear and create a general atmosphere of insecurity. Other minorities have also not been vocal about the need for a uniform civil code. They have maintained a silence which is to indicate that the uniform civil code is primarily a battle of will between the Hindus and Muslims. All Hindus want a uniform civil code and therefore, all Muslims do not want a uniform civil code. Both projections are incorrect; the question that is unanswered is how the issue of uniform civil code is addressed by other minorities. Not answering the same, amounts to playing politics with the national interest.

I am sorry to state that the role played by the national press and media has also been irresponsible. Hamid Dalwai, Asghar Ali Engineer and likes of Arif Mohammad Khan have not been called upon to stir public opinion. What Arif Mohammad Khan suffered in the aftermath of the Muslim Women's Bill is public knowledge. Their ideas are not publicized by the Press. Non-fundamentalist, reformative, nationalist and humanist views and the views of gender justice, need to be disseminated, for building a consensus for implementing a uniform civil code, which already almost exists in the state of Goa.

Minority Manipulation Virus

— Dr Pravin Togadia

It has been proven beyond doubt that Islamic forces have forcibly invaded many countries and civilizations. These forces have destroyed the existing culture, civilization and religion of almost every country they have attacked—converting the local population by force. In its history of the last 14 centuries, Islam occupied many countries in the world, some so completely that those countries have been declared 'officially Islamic' (Malaysia, Indonesia, Pakistan, Iran, Afghanistan etc). It has also set the target of converting those countries not under its occupation Dar-ul-Islam—lands ruled by Islam. According to Islam, lands that are ruled by non-Muslims, the 'infidels', are called Dar-ul-Harb, or 'land of war'. To achieve its goal, Islam has used force in the past and even now, the world is experiencing the same attitude and behaviour from the denizens of this faith. Among the prominent examples of this expansionist ideology are the Islamic terror attacks of 9/11 (2001) in New York and 26/11 (2008) in Mumbai.

The concept of minority, essentially, is an ultra-modern concept that suits a few recently created states which profess to adhere to the notion of democracy, but do not recognize each civilization's uniqueness. The concept as a political construct first gained currency in Europe after the First World War, when the concept of the nation-state grew in importance and the political boundaries of many countries were redefined to accommodate and protect those, who got displaced, as well as to protect the ethnicity of Europe. However, the basis of a minority then was language.

Bharat, because of its unique civilizational ethos, did not have to redefine the political boundaries of a nation-state. Then what is the reason for the concept of minority being used and misused today, not to help the really poor or needy, but solely to demean, degrade and dispossess the majority Hindus?

In order to understand the dangerous game behind minority appeasement in Bharat, it is essential to delve into the dictionary meaning of the word appeasement, which is to make someone calm or less hostile by agreeing to his demands. Therein lies the catch! It is amply clear from the definition of the term itself, that the group which today's politicos have been wooing, terming them a 'minority' is already hostile towards the nation named Bharat, to the citizens of the nation named Bharat and as a logical corollary—to the majority of Bharat. Why is this particular group hostile to Bharat? Because being hostile to all others who are not 'like them' or 'those who do not follow their faith' is a rule of their religion that does not accept the basic theory of nation. Their belief is of the rule of the Ummah—the rule of the Islamic community all over the world with no place for any nation-state!

Let us closely examine who really are these people who claim to be a 'poor minority' in Bharat (and in many other countries) It is the very set of people, who currently rule over 44 countries and for 14 centuries have attacked, encroached and ruled many more countries, destroying those countries' cultures, civilizations and cultural heritages, and are now using democracy as a new weapon to do the same again.

This is the real reason Muslims in Bharat claim to be 'the second-largest majority in Bharat'. Their unmistakable goal is to grab the political pie while assiduously claiming to be 'a poor underdeveloped minority'; they want to snatch the hard-earned wealth and the benefits earned by Bharat's majority, who truly work hard and are the ones who actually pay taxes.

There are other true minorities in Bharat—as there are in many other countries. For instance, many tribes in most countries are now on the verge of being extinguished. We come across such instances in the hilly and coastal regions of Bharat too. Some of these groups are trying to be a part of the new economy preserving their culture, while some others are being forced to convert—either through force by Islam or by allurement and force by Christianity. While the issue of conversions can be tackled at a humane and strategic level, Islamic invasion can never be countered democratically, as Islam does not believe in the concept of nation per se, nor does it believe in democracy. An SOS at this stage about Islamic invasion of Bharat and the world at large—and this does not mean historical invasion, but one that is taking place right now—is not an exaggeration.

The second largest majority in Bharat, which manipulates our kind-heartedness, democracy and untiring efforts at development by resorting to its time-tested tactics of feigned victimhood, must be clearly identified for what it actually is—usurper. It is a serious threat to Bharat's democracy, development, economic future, rich cultural heritage and unrivalled civilization. This is a warning to those who squander the nation's valuable resources on these surreptitious foes at the expense of the majority.

The shameless appeasement of the Muslim "minorities" is done with the sole purpose of garnering their votes. No political party is seen appeasing India's tribes or similar groups, which are the true victims of the industrial age and truly need help. In this process, successive regimes at the centre and the states, have kowtowed to an aggressive Islam. Kashmir, for instance, has been all but gifted to pan-Islam, with Assam and parts of many states not far behind. This debilitating and treacherous process is rapidly eroding the morale of our security forces, government officials, the working classes and the majority of our nation's youth. If these vote-hungry appeasement policies and actions are not halted at once, it will not take more than ten years for Bharat to be transformed into another Dar-ul-Islam.

The concept of a religious minority should have become a non-issue in Bharat. Instead, the most vocal and organized "minority" with undeniable extra-territorial loyalty, has been able to become the largest beneficiary group, at the expense of our nation and its long-term interests! What is the real motto of this ultra-vocal "minority"?

Islamic separatism, religious intolerance and anti-nationalism can rightly be called the credo of this "minority". Muslim minorities have perfected the art of exploiting vote-hungry politicians to manipulate, and subvert democratic freedoms. As a result, the virus of Muslim minority manipulation is spreading so rapidly in Bharat that the entire nation is in its grip.

The deadly cocktail of the opportunism of political parties, vote-bank policies falsely portrayed as development policies and Islamic separatism and anti-nationalism are eagerly supported by greedy politicians. It is also important to learn the stark fact that anti-nationalism is inherent in Islam, right from its very inception. Islam has never believed in the concept of nation.

That the Muslim minority manipulation (MMM) virus has already spread in Bharat is amply clear from its following symptoms:

1. Refusal to accept population control using the pretext c religion;
2. Refusal to accept a Uniform Civil Code citing religious e clusivity as a matter of right;
3. Incessant attacks on the Hindu majority;
4. Screaming victimhood whenever the majority reacts or r ates against attacks on itself, and co-opting the medi intelligentsia for this false campaign of victimhood;
5. Fleecing the nation's resources;
6. Taking to streets for any issue concerning Muslims all world, but remaining conspicuously invisible and de silent when Islamic jihadis attack Bharat. Of late, th minority has also begun indulging in display of fa patriotism, by lighting candles or exhibiting idol and Durga near the gates of their mosques.

Bharat is in mortal danger from the MMM virus, which is reaching uncontrollable proportions. From Kashmir to Assam, Kerala to Gujarat and Mumbai to Mewat, this virus has already caused nationwide destruction. Preventive measures like compulsory population control, ban on four marriages (sanctioned by Islam), scrapping of the special status to "minority" institutions and many such should have been taken in 1947. It is too late for these now.

To counter the dangerous and spiraling impact of Muslim appeasement and thereby of this deadly anti-national virus, we must compel the country's politicians to accept the universal truth: Muslim appeasement is an anti-national act. All voters must test their leaders on the parameters of the extent to which they are the victims of the MMM virus, and respond accordingly.

The opposing forces in Bharat must be clearly identified—national forces, which do not appease the MMM virus and therefore do not support separatism and anti-nationalism and the anti-national ones, who constantly appease the MMM virus and thereby support separatism and anti-nationalism.

Observe how many Muslim candidates were floated by the party you voted for twelve years back and how many are put up today? Ask where your tax money goes? How much comes to you and how much to the so-called minority? Observe closely if your chosen leader suddenly, and in a very glowing manner, starts talking about the great "development" he has done for these "minorities"... you will know for yourself if your leader has himself been afflicted with MMM virus!

Unless and until every majority voter makes a resolve that he/she will never vote for any candidate guilty of the above behavior and actions, Bharat's polity will never achieve the well-being of the nation.

In order to curtail the growth of this Muslim Minority Manipulation virus, the necessary—and fast becoming imperative—steps are doing away with minority provisions, scrapping of Articles 25 to 30 of the Constitution, implement of a Uniform Civil Code, abolition of Article 370 and disenfranchisement of this aggressive and anti-national "minority"!

Only if these steps are taken immediately, can Bharat (and all other freedom-loving and civilized countries) survive as nations and progress further. Bharat is an ancient nation with a rich cultural heritage and is also an intellectual superpower. But its present self-debilitating politics of appeasement of an implacable and hostile religious ideology will certainly take it down the path other civilizations have fallen and she will end up as one of the numerous Islamic caliphates. History can of course, repeat itself, but then why must we let the history of only the last 1,400 years, of the events of 1947 and later, be repeated? Why should we not repeat the history of ancient, developed, intellectually advanced and culturally rich Bharat?

Economic Consequences of Minority Appeasement

— Subramanian Swamy

Economic science teaches us that only in a transparently regulated competitive market system will the allocation of the nation's resources, for alternative uses, be optimal and yield maximum return on investment. This means giving to primacy, to merit.

However, those sections of society which have disabilities, which could be mental, physical, gender, or cognitive (which have been imposed on those sections by circumstances or by prolonged social discrimination) are entitled to affirmative action to compensate for these disabilities, to empower them to compete but with a handicap. This is how we can achieve inclusive development.

By this criterion, only Scheduled Castes, Scheduled Tribes and women are entitled to by-pass the usual competitive selection by merit. To offer reservations and quotas to Muslims and Christians is however, unjustified because these two communities do not suffer from any imposed disabilities. On the contrary, they were part of the ruling classes of India—for a total of 1000 years, and therefore could not be victims of any social or political oppression. In any event, affirmative action is bad economics too, because it leads to sub-optimization. It is pure and simple appeasement, therefore, to recommend or advocate reservations or quotas for these two communities, as in fact the Sachar and Ranganath Mishra Commissions have done.

The question that I have repeatedly asked those who are appeasing the Muslims today is: Why have the Muslims, who ruled India for over eight hundred years and belonged to the privileged ruling class (even during the hundred and fifty years of British Raj, while subjecting the Hindus to unspeakable tortures, violence, rape and suppression) become socially handicapped compared to Hindus? To date, I have not received even a semblance of an answer.

Sixty years ago, Dr B R Ambedkar had warned us about the terrible consequences of appeasement. Analyzing the attitude of the Congress Party in 1940 to the demands of Mohammed Ali Jinnah, he said the party was adopting a policy of appeasement.

In his book *Thoughts on Pakistan*, which I believe must be read by every patriot, Dr Ambedkar had said:

> Appeasement [of Jinnah] means to offer to buy off the aggressor by conniving at or collaborating with him in the rape, murder and arson on innocent Hindus who happen for the moment to be the victims of his displeasure.
>
> On the other hand settlement means laying down the bounds which neither party to it can transgress. Appeasement has no limits to the demands and aspirations of the aggressor. Settlement does.
>
> The second thing the Congress has failed to realize is, that

> the policy of concession has increased their aggressiveness and what is worse, the Muslims interpret these concessions as a sign of defeatism on the part of the Hindus and the absence of will to resist. This policy of appeasement will involve the Hindus in the same fearful situation in which the Allies found themselves as a result of the policy of appeasement which they adopted towards Hitler.

Dr Ambedkar, therefore, felt that the creation of a separate Islamic state of Pakistan with transfer of population could be a preferable settlement that could end the Hindu-Muslim problem in the sub-continent. However, the Congress Party, which was handed power by the British, did not heed Dr Ambedkar's sage advice. Today, after six decades, it is too late to implement Dr Ambedkar's suggestion. Instead, I suggest that we accept as our brothers and sisters those Muslims and Christians who proudly acknowledge that their ancestors were Hindus. They accept that change in religion does not mean change in their ancestral Hindu culture. Those who do not acknowledge and accept this should be placed on par with NRIs when it comes to citizenship rights.

Prime Minister Dr Manmohan Singh's ridiculous statement that 'Muslims have the first charge on our resources', revealed that he too had contracted the 'M' virus. Minorityism or the M virus unsettles the rationality of Indian political leaders, and makes them favour minorities even if not required, on the principles of equity.

Compassion for deprived minorities and their concerns is a noble human rights value. But being fixated on Muslims and Christians, as the only minorities of concern, even if they are majorities in pockets e.g., in Kashmir and Northeast India, is debilitating.

In such lop-sided minorityism, Hindus wherever and whenever

they are in a minority do not have the same rights, as recent history in Kashmir and Northeast has proved. The fact that Hindus in these areas are being butchered, raped, driven out, forcibly converted does not concern Dr Manmohan Singh. Muslims and Christians as minorities, are not entitled to 'first charge' because sequentially Muslims and Christians have been ruling classes for a thousand years while Hindus were brutalized. Only SC and STs are entitled to first charge, and that too for one generation.

Political parties, which have been swearing by 'secularism' all these years, because of vote-bank minorityism, have failed to persuade the masses that what they advocate is good for the country. Secularism as defined and propagated today in India has been reduced to minorityism or minority appeasement. It is only the Hindus who appease Muslims and Christians in the majority pockets of India, without that favour being returned anywhere else in the world. The question today is not whether secularism is flawed but whether we should conceptually redefine secularism to make it acceptable to the masses in the country. Such a re-defined concept must be harmonized with the concept of an Indian identity, which requires that India be regarded as Hindustan, i.e., a nation of Hindus and those others who proudly accept Hindus as their ancestors. In this context, Indianness means 'Hindutva'. Thus, Indian identity rests on two pillars: India as Hindustan and Indianness as Hindutva.

The country's first Prime Minister Jawaharlal Nehru and his followers gave the concept of secularism an anti-Hindu content. For example, personal and inheritance laws would be legislated for Hindus and subject to judicial review, but not for Muslims and Christians. Clearly, Manmohan Singh's 'M virus' has its roots in Nehruism. Even at public functions, cultural symbolism such as lighting a lamp to inaugurate a conference or breaking a coconut to launch a project was regarded as 'anti-secular'. A conceptual void will linger until we not only reject minorityism but also develop a concept of secularisn that is in harmony with the national imperative of Hindutva and the nation as Hindustan.

To fill this void, we need to develop a concept of secularism by which an Indian citizen could comprehend how he or she should bond "secularly" with another citizen of a different religion, language or region and feel as a fellow countryman. Indians, by instinct, cannot accept the idea that India is what the British had put together, and that the country was just a body administratively incorporated. Instead, Bharat-Mata has a soul which Deendayal Upadhyaya had called Chiti, something that the anglicized Nehru failed to even comprehend, much less accept. The ridiculous idea that India is a nation fostered by British rule, propagated even today by Jawaharl Nehru University historians, has simply no takers amongst India

Only by using religious symbols can this void be filled. I is 83 per cent Hindu, and all folklore in this religion is pan-Inc Thus, it is easy for the masses of all Hindustanis to understand share religious bonding. The events of the Ramayana narra span the Punjab to Sri Lanka. The Mahabharata's events cove region from Assam to Gujarat. Adi Shankara connected Ker Kashmir. This not need alienate Muslims and Christians if proudly accept that their ancestors were Hindus. The pro arises only if the Muslims and Christians identify themselve foreign invaders.

Minorityism has a debilitating effect on national identity and integrity. It enables Muslim men to resist family planning by keeping their women vulnerable to divorce in an instant, and hence, women have no voice in how many children they will bear. Muslim men know that a uniform civil code will materialize under regimes hankering after their vote-bank. Christian missionaries, under this very minorityism, have a free hand to conduct money-induced religious conversion. They have scant regard from where that money comes and what ethical and moral norms they have to violate for it.

For example, Mother Theresa shocked the conscience of all genuinely secular-minded persons when she wrote directly to Judge Lance Ito of Los Angeles Court on behalf of a known fraud and embezzler, Charles Keating, who was facing prosecution for stealing $252 million from 17,000 pensioners, retail stock holders and insurance premiums by selling them bogus bonds of his company. He had donated $5 million (Rs 25 crore) to Missionaries of Charity, Kolkata headed by Mother Theresa, and that was enough for her to write to Judge Ito directly asking him not to convict Keating! Her words to Judge Ito were even more astounding: "Please look into your heart as you sentence Charles Keating—and do what Jesus would do."

To his credit, Judge Ito ignored Teresa's sanctimonious homilies, sent Keating to jail for years, and also imposed a huge fine. He, however, asked the Public Prosecutor (Deputy District Attorney in US) Paul W Turley to reply to Mother Theresa. Turley turned Mother Theresa's plea on her by posing a question "You asked Judge Ito to do what Jesus would do. I submit the same challenge to you: Ask yourself what Jesus would do if he were given the fruits of a crime; what Jesus would do if he were in possession of money that had been stolen; what Jesus would do if he were being exploited by a thief to ease his conscience?" Then came Turley's punch line: "I submit that Jesus would promptly and unhesitatingly return the stolen property to its rightful owners. You should do the same."

Then Turley implored Mother Theresa: "You have been given money by Mr Keating that he has been convicted of stealing by fraud. Do not keep the money. Return it to those who worked for it and earned it! If you contact me I will put you in direct contact with the rightful owners of the property now in your possession." (Extracted from Hitchens Christopher: The Missionary Position: Mother Theresa in Theory and Practice). Of course, Mother Theresa felt no such moral compulsion, ignored Turley and kept Keating's tainted and stolen gift of $5 million.

Hence, we Hindus, in the name of secularism and '*vasudeva kutambakkam*' must not fall prey to pious-looking foreign ladies dressed in saris and talking about a 'universal God.' Remember, when Ravana came to abduct Sita, he came dressed as a pious *sanyasi*, and not as his true self.

Likewise, minorityism is a recipe for national disintegration and disaster. Capitulationist Hindus are paving the way for this to happen. The only antidote is a *virat* (mighty) Hindutva. The present UPA regime is hell-bent on protecting the interests of only Muslims and Christians by its minorityism. In 2005, a group of Mizos were discovered by Jewish scholars as a lost tribe. The Mizos also confirmed that their practices were formerly Jewish but were converted forcibly to Christianity by British colonialists. They desired to return to the Jewish faith. Therefore, in November 2005, Israel decided to dispatch some Rabbis to Aizwal to conduct the necessary re-conversion ceremonies. But the "secular" Dr Manmohan Singh intervened—upon orders from Sonia Gandhi —to ask the MEA to cancel the Rabbis' visa and inform Israel that "Government of India does not approve of such conversion activities."

First, we need to be clear about the concept of minority before we can discuss minority rights. It is essential hence to understand how Muslims and Christians came to he regarded as 'minorities' in India. The word minority has a substantive meaning only if special protection in the Constitution is to be provided. Such protection is required for a minority in order to be compensated for some historically acquired or imposed disability. Otherwise it would be meaningless to have a discourse on minorities at all, much less waste public money on a Commission of Inquiry.

The present practice in India is to regard any group of less than 50 per cent of the population—except Hindus (e.g., in Kashmir) as minorities. This is ridiculous. Numbers are not a sufficient basis for defining a minority. The Whites of South Africa are numerically less, but cannot be treated as "minorities" deserving of special protection, reservations or affirmative action. Parsis, in India despite being a microscopic minority numerically, have consistently refused to ask for or accept any Constitutional safeguards as they have never felt disabled (for centuries) in a Hindu-dominated society. They are, therefore, not a minority in the constitutional or statutory dispensation.

Strange as it may sound, there is no definition of minority in the Indian Constitution [although Articles 29 and 30 make provisions for a minority, religious and linguistic), nor is there a definition in United Nations Resolutions or a universally-accepted definition in international law.

Some countries such as Thailand and Brazil refuse to accept concept of 'minorities' in their country. These nations had told the UN Sub-Commission on Prevention of Discrimination and Protection of Minorities that they have no minorities to notify, despite being a multi-religious, multi-racial society.

In 2001, an 11-judge Constitutional Bench, delivered a judgment on the question of minority rights in education [T M A Pai Foundation case], but did not define the term "minority". What they did do was to opine that minorities are not to be defined nationally but state-wise, thus overturning their 1971 DAV College judgment. Subsequent judgments of the Supreme Court, such as delivered by a 5-judge Constitutional Bench in 2003 in the Islamic Academy case, and the 7-judge Constitutional Bench in 2005 in the Inamdar case have also not defined the concept of minority.

In 1992, India's Parliament enacted the National Commission for Minorities Act, but did not define a minority in it. Section 2 (C) of the Act merely states that minority is what the Government of India will notify in the Gazette!! The Government has notified, without reason or explanation, Muslims, Christians, Sikhs and Parsis as religious minorities, without specifying any reason for doing so. Even the State Minorities Commissions have not bothered to define minorities.

In other words, the nation has been discussing "minority rights" for the last sixty years without defining what or who can be minorities. How can we identify minorities if we do not have a definition of the term?

Hence, I shall begin with my definition of minority and then discuss what their rights can be in, the context of national integrity. In this connection, it is appropriate to quote from the judgment of the 3-judge Supreme Court bench in Bal Patil versus the Union of India case, delivered by Justice Dharmadhikari in 2005:

> Such claims to minority status based on religion, would increase the fond hope of various sections of the people in getting special protections, privileges and treatment as part of the constitutional guarantee. Encouragement to such fissiparous tendencies would be a serious jolt to the secular structure of constitutional democracy. We should guard against making our country akin to a theocratic State based on multinationalism.

What we can therefore hold now is that if a group is numerically small, and substantially below 50 per cent of the population, then although it has the necessary attributes of a minority, that attribute is not sufficient for it to be declared a minority for the purpose of constitutional or statutory protection. Such a group must have sufficient other attributes as well, to be identified as a minority.

Based on the circumstances arising out of the Indian legacy, and in recognition of defining events of Indian history, I would define a 'Minority' in India as:

"A collective of Indian citizens, constituting a numerical minority and situated in a non-dominant position in society, endowed with characteristics which differ from those of the majority, having suffered from imposed deprivation over a long period and thus have acquired disabilities, are a minority if these disabilities cannot be removed except by providing special constitutional protection and facilities for affirmative action."

That is, to qualify as a minority under the Constitution of India, it is required that such a group be in a non-dominant position in society, have suffered deprivation for a long period, to have acquired disabilities which cannot be removed except by special constitutional protection, such as reservations in jobs and educational institutions.

By this definition, the scheduled castes and scheduled tribes would constitute a minority even if they are a part of the numerical majority Hindu community. Their disabilities cannot be removed except by specific affirmative action such as reservation in jobs, education, and in legislatures. Backward castes of the Hindu community also suffer disabilities, but these can be removed by special arrangements of education facilities and financial assistance. But due to our political folly and selfishness, these backward castes have been given reservations in jobs and education which cannot now be taken away except by persuasion, in the future. When world-class primary and secondary education can be provided to all, it is conceivable that the youth of the backward castes would prefer to compete rather than advance by availing of quotas. Since the Indian DNA structure is the same for all castes, hence, competing on merit, if equally empowered, is possible for the backward castes.

But Muslims and Christians cannot be considered as

minorities in Indian society because their disabilities are not an outcome of any deprivation imposed on them. In fact, Muslims and Christians, like the Whites of South Africa, have been the ruling classes in India for a long period. Sequentially, these two religious groups have ruled India for over a thousand years, during which period they practiced religious apartheid against the Hindus. Hence, for the cause of national integrity, patriotic Indians should resist with all their might, any attempt to introduce quotas in jobs, education, or in anything else, for the benefit of Muslims and Christians. Those Muslims and Christians who consider themselves Indians should also, like the Parsis, reject any offer by mischievous politicians to introduce quotas for them. Instead, they should ask for world-class primary and secondary education to empower them to compete on a level playing field with the rest of the society.

Whatever has now been incorporated in the Constitution as minority rights, cannot be taken away. Articles 29 and 30 are part of the Basic Structure of the Constitution and cannot be amended. Hence, minorities will continue to have the right for example, to administer their own educational institutions. But as the Supreme Court has held in the Islamic Academy case, the unfettered right to administer does not include the right to mal-administer. Hence, minority-run educational institutions, including unaided ones, must be subject to obtaining government approval for curriculum standards, faculty quality, and basic infrastructure that should be common to all. Sooner or later, we must require that all students, including Muslims and Christians, learn Sanskritised Hindi, whose vocabulary should be progressively Sanskritised till Hindi becomes indistinguishable from Sanskrit. Our long-term link language has to be Sanskrit, because its vocabulary is in a large measure in every language. Even Tamil draws 40 per cent of its vocabulary from Sanskrit.

The goal of minority rights has to be to further social justice. Towards this end, we must strive for equal and high quality educational opportunity and create a mindset for national unity and integration. Quotas and reservations are essential for Scheduled Castes and Tribes, but here too the concept of creamy layer must operate. We cannot accept special rights for religious minorities of Muslims and Christians, just as we cannot for Brahmins although they are as poor as backward Muslims and Christians. The logic is the same—those who have been the ruling classes cannot claim minority status in the constitutional matrix of the nation.

In my opinion, Muslims and Christians should look inward and analyze, why after being the ruling classes of India for a thousand years, they now need reservations to compete with hapless Hindus who have suffered huge prosecution, discrimination and impoverishment at the hands of Muslim and Christian rulers. On the contrary, instead of giving reservations to Muslims and Christians, Hindus should demand that Muslims and Christians atone for past atrocities committed by their rulers on Hindus or alternatively, disown their long-gone rulers, and proudly declare themselves to be the descendents of Hindus.

Islamization begins when there are sufficient Muslims in a country to agitate for their religious privileges, as Dr Peter Hammond has observed in his many writings. When politically correct, tolerant, and culturally diverse societies agree to Muslim demands for their religious privileges, many other unsavoury components tend to creep in as well.

As long as the Muslim population remains around or under 2 per cent and the non Muslim majority remains cohesive in any given country, Muslims will be for the most part a 'peace-loving' minority, and not a threat to other citizens. This is the case in:

United States—Muslim 0.6%

Australia—Muslim 1.5%

Canada—Muslim 1.9%

China—Muslim 1.8%

Italy—Muslim 1.5%

Norway—Muslim 1.8%

At two per cent to five per cent, they begin to proselytize from other ethnic minorities and disaffected groups, often with major recruiting from the jails and among street gangs. This is happening in:

Denmark—Muslim 2%

Germany—Muslim 3.7%

United Kingdom—Muslim 2.7%

Spain—Muslim 4%

Thailand—Muslim 4.6%

From five per cent on, they exercise an inordinate influence in proportion to their percentage of the population. For example, they will push for the introduction of *halal* (clean by Islamic standards) food, thereby securing food preparation jobs for Muslims. They will increase pressure on supermarket chains to stock *halal* meat on their shelves—along with threats for failure to comply. This is occurring in:

France—Muslim 8%

Philippines—Muslim 5%

Sweden—Muslim 5%

Switzerland—Muslim 4.3%

The Netherlands—Muslim 5.5%

Trinidad & Tobago—Muslim 5.8%

At this point, they will work to get the ruling government to allow them to rule themselves (within their ghettos) under Sharia, the Islamic Law. The ultimate goal of Islamists is to establish Sharia over the entire world.

When Muslims approach 10 per cent of the population, they tend to increase lawlessness as a means of complaint about their conditions. In Paris, we are already witnessing car-burnings. Any non-Muslim action offends Islam, and results in uprisings and threats, such as in Amsterdam, with opposition to Mohammed cartoons and films about Islam. Such tensions are seen daily, particularly in Muslim sections, in:

Guyana—Muslim 10%

India—Muslim 13.4%

Israel —Muslim 16%

Kenya—Muslim 10%

Russia—Muslim 15%

When Muslims reach 20 per cent, host nations can expect hair-trigger rioting, jihad militia formations, sporadic killings, and the burnings of places of worship of non-Muslim religions, such as in Ethiopia with the Muslim population at 32.8 per cent.

At 40 per cent, nations experience widespread massacres, chronic terror attacks, and ongoing militia warfare, such as in:

Bosnia—Muslim 40%

Chad—Muslim 53.1%

Lebanon—Muslim 59.7%

From 60 per cent, nations experience unfettered persecution of non-believers of all other religions (including non-conforming Muslims), sporadic ethnic cleansing (genocide), use of Sharia as a weapon, and *Jizya*, the tax placed on infidels, such as in:

Albania—Muslim 70%

Malaysia—Muslim 60.4%

Qatar—Muslim 77.5%

Sudan—Muslim 70%

After 80 per cent, non-Muslims, who will be an intimidated minority, can expect daily intimidation and violent jihad, State-run ethnic cleansing, and even genocide, as these Muslim nations drive out the infidels, and move towards becoming 100 per cent Muslim, as has been experienced in:

Bangladesh—Muslim 83%

Egypt—Muslim 90%

Gaza—Muslim 98.7%

Indonesia—Muslim 86.1%

Iran—Muslim 98%

Iraq—Muslim 97%

Jordan—Muslim 92%

Morocco—Muslim 98.7%

Pakistan—Muslim 97%

Palestine—Muslim 99%

Syria—Muslim 90%

Tajikistan—Muslim 90%

Turkey—Muslim 99.8%

United Arab Emirates—Muslim 96%

A 100 per cent Muslim land will usher in the peace of '*Dar-ul-Islam*'—the Islamic House of Peace. In such a state, there's supposed to be peace, because everybody is a Muslim. Madrassas are the only schools, and the *Quran* is the only word, such as in:

Afghanistan—Muslim 100%

Saudi Arabia—Muslim 100%

Somalia—Muslim 100%

Yemen—Muslim 100%

The reality is that this mythical peace is never achieved, as in these 100 per cent states the most radical Muslims intimidate and kill less radical Muslims, for a variety of reasons adduced on the basis of the *Shariat*.

It is important to understand that in some countries, with well under 100 per cent Muslim populations, such as France, the minority Muslim populations live in ghettos, within which they are 100 per cent Muslim, and within which they live by Sharia. The national police do not even enter these ghettos. There are no national courts, nor schools, nor non-Muslim religious facilities. Muslims in non-Muslim nations do not integrate into the host community at all.

In India, proposals for appeasement through reservations for Dalit Muslims and Christians have been in two pending petitions in the Supreme Court, while a third from the All-India Christian Federation has been admitted at the beginning of the year. The apex court has asked the centre to reply to the plea that Dalits in the Zoroastrian, Jain, Christian and Muslim communities be granted Scheduled Caste (SC) status. Already, the report of the National Commission for Religious and Linguistic Minorities, popularly known as the Ranganath Mishra Commission, has stirred a hornet's nest with its recommendations.

Submitted in May 2007, it was not tabled in Parliament until it got leaked to the media. The government had to give in to pressures from a section of the Members of Parliament. It says that quotas in government jobs, education and welfare schemes should be extended to all religious minorities, including the Hindus where they are in a minority. In the matter of the criteria for identifying backward classes, "there should be absolutely no discrimination whatsoever between the majority community and the minorities." Therefore, "the criteria now applied, for this purpose to the majority community...must be unreservedly applied to all the minorities."

The Congress' election manifesto had boasted of having pioneered reservations for minorities in Kerala, Karnataka and Andhra Pradesh. However, its government is equivocal over the recommendation of a 15 per cent quota for minorities, 10 per cent of it for Muslims and the rest to the other minorities. It has made it amply clear that it is in no hurry to act on the recommendations which would only promote religious conversion. Christian and Muslim organizations are vociferous in demanding immediate implementation.

But a number of Dalit organizations in Tamil Nadu also have warned of agitations if the Mishra report is implemented. The Mishra report has suggested that if the 15 per cent reservation is not possible due to an "insurmountable difficulty", then, in the

27 per cent Other Backward Classes (OBC) quota, an 8.4 per cent sub-quota should be earmarked for minorities, based on the Mandal Commission's estimate that the minorities constitute 8.4 per cent of the total OBC population. The government's statement that it is considering this possibility is not going to be welcomed by the OBC leaders of the majority community.

"*Dalits in the Muslim and Christian Communities: A Status Report on Current Social Scientific Knowledge*" prepared for the National Commission for Minorities by Satish Deshpande (with the assistance of Geetika Bapna) and submitted in January 2008, analyzed data from the National Sample Survey Organization to map the economic well-being of these 'Dalit' sections of the two communities, and compare their situation with that of non-Dalits in their own communities and Dalits in other communities. It concludes, among other things, that there can be no doubt whatsoever that Dalit Muslim Section (DMS) and Dalit Christians (DC) are invariably regarded as 'socially inferior' communities by their co-religionists. This is a severe indictment of Islam and Christianity.

The other conclusions of this status report are also significant. In terms of poverty, DMS are the worst among all Dalits in both rural and urban areas; DCs are moderately better off than other Dalits, except Dalit Sikhs who are even better off. In intra-community comparisons, DMS are only slightly worse off than non-Dalit Muslims but that is because the Muslim community as a whole tends to be very badly off compared to other communities.

This reveals that even after conversion to Islam or Christianity, Dalits are not able to improve their lot. That is why

Dr Ambedkar was farsighted to convert to Buddhism instead of Islam or Christianity.

Some radical Muslim leaders, especially at forums where foreign journalists are present, proclaim unabashedly that Muslims in India are living in perpetual threat and are being treated as second-class citizens in this country. If that were indeed so, these leaders need to explain how over two crore Bangladeshi Muslims and over a lakh Muslims immigrated into India illegally from Pakistan at the risk of being killed by BSF or the Army at the border, and another 80,000 Muslims who came from Pakistan on valid visas just vanished and got absorbed in India, giving up their "Free From Fear" environment and first-class citizenship status in Bangladesh and Pakistan respectively, to court a life of "perpetual fear and a status of second class citizenship" in India?

As for the supposed Islamic utopia, let the apologists explain, as Konrad Elst in his book India's '*Only Communalist*', pertinently points out that successive UN reports on the State of the Arab countries have documented how in spite of their God-given abundant oil wealth, they are hopelessly behind, in practically every respect of human endeavour: human rights, gender equality, entrepreneurship, original research, inventions patented, Internet access per head, books published, sales of books, foreign books translated, etc, not to mention democracy.

Therefore, religion-based quotas and reservation are certainly not the cure for a backwardness, that is not imposed, but caused by an unsafeguarded and unregulated educational system. If state-owned schools have a high absenteeism of teachers, and even higher student drop-out rate because of poor employment opportunities at the semi-skilled level, backwardness will be the economic consequence. It is wrong, however, to identify this as socially imposed.

We also have to demolish some 'dominant' caste myths about our economy as well. Caste groups are not uniform monoliths. Incomes across caste groups differ widely across various states. There is also false notion that differences in income automatically imply discrimination, and therefore affirmative action is called for. Apart from the impact of the "state" of development on income levels, differences between castes are largely explained by education, by the industry/service of employment, by whether an individual is situated in a rural area or a small town or a metro, and the list can go on.

There's education as well. A large part of the higher income levels in urban settings are probably also a reflection of higher education, not just location because it needs sophisticated econometrics, and even that can go wrong, a fact often ignored.

In the case of Muslims, where the government hopes to fix things through an Equal Opportunities Commission, it's worth keeping in mind that nearly 90 per cent live in rural areas (64 per cent) and small towns; Muslims have the highest proportion of households who are self-employed in non-agricultural occupations (25.7 per cent versus 16.2 for Hindus) and the least who are salaried (13.1 per cent versus 18.8 per cent for all Hindus).

The moral of the story is that it is not so much imposed disabilities as it is about urbanization, industrialization and education. Not that changing the scenario is easy either. The agitation against land acquisition in Uttar Pradesh shows the limits to the pace of urbanization.

The lack of Hindu unity and the determined bloc voting in elections by Muslims and Christians has, however, created a significantly large leverage for these two religious communities in economic, social and foreign policymaking. Thus, although a Uniform Civil Code is a Directive Principle of State Policy in the Constitution, it is taboo to ask for it because of this leverage. It is not as if Muslims will not accept uniform laws when it suits them, even if it is against the *Shariat*. For example, Muslims accept a uniform criminal code under the IPC even though it infringes the *Shariat*, but resist a uniform civil code because it violates the *Shariat*. These contradictions are permitted for Muslims by the Mullahs because India is considered *Dar-ul-Harb* (Land of the Enemy).

Accordingly, the Muslim leadership deploys its leverage where it is tactically advantageous. This leverage exists despite the people of India who declare in the Census that they are adherents of religions which were born on Indian soil. Hindus, Sikhs, Buddhists, and Jains constituted 83.21 per cent of the total Indian population (as of last Census in 2001).

In 1941, this proportion, adjusted for Partition, was 84.44 per cent. But this figure hides the fact that Hindus, resident in undivided Pakistan, have migrated to post-Partition India which is why the share of Hindus and co-religionists has barely reduced since 1941. In the area now called Bangladesh, Hindus were 30 per cent in 1941. In 2001, they are less than 8 per cent. In Pakistan of today, Hindus were 20 per cent in 1941, and less than 2 per cent in 2001. Such religious cleansing has, however, not been noticed by the world at large! When Hindus themselves do not care, why should the world take notice?

If the figures are adjusted for this migration, then in the five decades 1951-2001, Hindus have lost more 3 per cent points in the share of Indian population, while Muslims have increased their share by about 3 per cent. What is even more significant is that Hindus have lost 12 per cent points since 1881, and the loss in share has begun to accelerate since 1971 partly due to illegal migration of Muslims from Bangladesh.

The current scenario of minority appeasement is that Muslims and Christians together, even though less than 16 per cent of the voters, vote en bloc. Hindus despite being over 83 per cent of the voters are hopelessly divided and amorphous. Hence, unless a Hindu bloc vote emerges, to the extent of at least 35 per cent of the 83 per cent, minority appeasement will continue at the expense of Hindus.

The mother of all problems amongst Muslims is the lack of secondary and higher education. Leave alone the Muslim women, even the literacy rates of Muslim males are way below the national average. This is so, despite the fact that community-wise, the percentage of Muslims living in urban areas is 50 per cent higher in comparison to the percentage of Hindus, and the chances of obtaining higher education are more easily available to urban dwellers as against the rural folks.

Therefore, rather than hanker after reservations as a panacea, the Muslim community in India must undergo a cultural revolution to develop a healthy attitude to secular and cognitive arts and sciences and to gender equality. Reservations and quotas are emphatically not the right medicine for the Muslim community's current backwardness.

National Commission for Minorities

— Shreerang Godbole

The position of religious minorities in Independent India was a question that had received the attention of some of the tallest leaders of our freedom movement. The Hindu nationalist position on the matter was made abundantly clear by Veer Savarkar. In his Presidential address to the 20th session of the Hindu Mahasabha (Nagpur, 1938), Savarkar said: "The Hindus will ever be ready to grant equal rights and representation to all minor communities in India in legislatures and services, civil and political life in proportion to population and merit. The Hindus, although they are in overwhelming majority will still waive their right of claiming any preferential treatment and special prerogatives which, in fact, in every other nation are due to the majority community. But the Hindus will never tolerate the absurd and unheard of claims of the minorities to have any preferential treatment, weightages or special favours over and above what the majority community obtains." Sardar Vallabbhai Patel had said, "In the long run it would be in the interests of all to forget that there is anything like a majority or a minority in this country and that in India there is only one community."

Probably, it may not be 'politically correct' to quote Savarkar or Patel in the current political climate; one can also quote Jawaharlal Nehru in this regard. In his address to the Constituent Assembly during the debate on minority rights, Nehru had said: "(In) a full-blooded democracy, if you seek to give safeguards to a minority, and a relatively small minority, you isolate it. Maybe you protect it to a slight extent, but at what cost? At the cost of isolating it and keeping it away from the main current in which the majority is going—I am talking on the political plane of course—at the cost of forfeiting that inner sympathy and fellow-feeling with the majority."

The Indian State has steadily moved away from the vision of 'One Nation, One People'. India has a determined and astute religious minority that is fully alive to its long-term political and strategic objectives. It also has a clueless majority led by a short-sighted intellectual and political class. Both these factors have ensured that institutional mechanisms continue to be created by the State to address the ever-escalating imaginary grievances of the minorities. In some cases, these mechanisms were simply handed over to the minorities on a platter though no corresponding demand had been made by them. Over the years, these mechanisms have become firmly entrenched and in fact, given more teeth. They now threaten to undermine the Indian State itself.

The following is an ever-expanding list of government programmes and institutions dealing exclusively with the minorities:

1. Ministry of Minority Affairs, Government of India (established 2006)
2. Prime Minister's new (2006) 15-Point Programme for the Development of Minorities
   (under Ministry of Minority Affairs)
3. National Integration Council, presently with the Ministry of Home Affairs. Communal Harmony Award
4. Office of the Commissioner for Linguistic Minorities
   (under Ministry of Minority Affairs)
   National Commission for Minorities
   (under Ministry of Minority Affairs)
   Central Wakf Council (under Ministry of Minority Affairs)
   Maulana Azad Educational Foundation
   (under Ministry of Minority Affairs)
   National Minorities Development and Finance Corporation (under Ministry of Minority Affairs)
5. Haj Committee presently with Ministry of External Affairs
6. (a) Maulana Azad National Urdu University, presently with the Ministry of HRD
   (b) National Council for Promotion of Urdu Language
   (c) Madrassa Modernization Programme
   (d) National Commission for Minority Educational Institutions (NCMEI), established 2004

The National Commission for Minorities (NCM) is one of the oldest institutional mechanisms created by the Indian State to 'safeguard the interests of the minorities.' The NCM is a classic case of an institution being created for minorities without any corresponding demand from them. The NCM also exemplifies how a Frankenstein created by the Indian State continues to be invested with ever-increasing powers such that it now aspires to become 'a State within a State'. The NCM is also a depressing example of the abject failure of the so-called Hindu nationalist political leadership to stand up to the minority-appeasement politics of the secularist political class Genesis and growth of the NCM.

The forerunners of the NCM were the state-level Minorities Commissions established by the state governments in Uttar Pradesh, Bihar and Gujarat by ruling political dispensations of different ideological hues.

The first-ever Minorities Commission was established in 1960 in Uttar Pradesh by a Congress government under Dr Sampurnanand. The state government went ahead with an executive order to that effect despite misgivings about the constitutional tenability and political advisability of such a step. Ironically, Dr Sampurnanand was a devout Hindu, indeed a Hindi and Sanskrit scholar who also brought in a law for cow-protection in UP. If proof is needed that a devout Hindu need not necessarily be a politically conscious Hindu, this is one! The one-member Minorities Commission was expanded in 1974 into a ten-member body.

The Congress government in Bihar set up a multi-member Minorities Commission in 1971. This was reconstituted by the Janata Party government under Karpoori Thakur in November 1977 so that the chief minister became chairman. The Karpoori

Thakur government went a step further and constituted district-level Minorities Standing Committees.

In November 1977, the Janata Party government in Gujarat under Babubhai Patel set up a State Minorities High Powered Committee.

The idea of a national-level Minorities Commission was mentioned in the manifesto of the Janata Party during the 1977 general elections. Interestingly, the Draft Committee of the manifesto included L K Advani besides three socialists and one Gandhian. The Janata Party manifesto promised "to make suitable institutional arrangements for the protection of the constitutional and civil rights of the minorities and other weaker sections of the society."

After the Janata Party assumed power in 1977, a semi-government organization called the Minorities Commission was born in Delhi. It was piloted by then Home Minister Chaudhary Charan Singh and had the blessings of Prime Minister Morarji Desai. On 12 January 1978, the Union Home Ministry notified a Government Resolution[1] that said,

> "Despite the safeguards provided in the Constitution and the laws in force, there persists among the minorities a feeling of inequality and discrimination. In order to preserve secular traditions and to promote national integration, the Government of India attaches the highest importance to the enforcement of safeguards provided for the minorities and is of the firm view that effective institutional arrangements are urgently required for the enforcement and implementation of all the safeguards provided, for the minorities in the Constitution, in the Central and State laws and in government policies and administrative schemes enunciated from

time to time. The Government of India has, therefore, resolved to set up a Minorities Commission to safeguard the interests of the minorities whether based on religion or language" (In 1988, the Commission's Charter was amended to exclude linguistic minorities from its purview.)

Presently, there is clamour for conferring constitutional status to the NCM. What is not widely known is that such a status had been envisaged by the Morarji Government from the very beginning! On 3 August 1978, the government introduced in the Lok Sabha, the Constitution (forty-sixth) Amendment Bill 1978, which among other things made room for a constitutionally sanctioned Minorities Commission to "inspire greater confidence among the minorities." There was severe criticism from several legal and constitutional experts. Among them, V P Bharatiya called the Commission a "Phoenix" and condemned the government for "engrafting this foreign organism to the equality postulate of the Constitution." Though the Bill lapsed, the Morarji Government was undeterred. It introduced the Constitution (fifty-first) Amendment Bill 1979 which again fell due to lack of support. The Morarji Government made another unsuccessful attempt in that direction in a specially extended Lok Sabha session. Mercifully for the Hindus, his government had to chicken out after being slapped with a no-confidence motion.

It is noteworthy that former Chief Justice of India M H Beg who headed the Minorities Commission from 1981 to 1988 had in his very first report forcefully recommended that "the Minorities Commission should be replaced with or merged into a National Integration-cum-Human Rights Commission." Chairman Justice

Beg repeated and elaborated upon this recommendation in the next Annual report of the Minorities Commission. He even put forth the idea of replacing the Minorities Commission with a National Integration-cum-Human Rights Commission at a Conference of State Minorities Commissions and Boards held in Delhi in January 1984.

Though the Congress is perceived—and often rightly so—of being guilty of minority appeasement, the fact is that the successive Congress Governments under Indira Gandhi and Rajiv Gandhi had no plans to give either constitutional or even ordinary legislative support to the Commission or to even arm it with the powers exercisable under the Commissions of Inquiry Act, 1952. This was confirmed by official statements made by the Union Welfare Minister in the two Houses of Parliament on 25 November and 2 December 1988, saying that there was no justification for such demands. The Congress first promised to accord Constitutional status to the Commission before the 1991 general elections. But that was to come later.

A proposal to grant statutory status to the Minorities Commission was made in the election manifesto of the National Front led by V P Singh. In pursuance of this promise, the V P Singh-led regime planned to confer statutory and even constitutional status to the Minorities Commission. The Constitution (Sixty-Fifth Amendment) Act 1990 did not, however, equate the Minorities Commission with the National Commission for Scheduled Castes and Scheduled Tribes. As per the statement made by Ram Vilas Paswan in the Lok Sabha in 1992, this could not be done because "the men of BJP were with us in the government" in 1990.

The present NCM is a creature that came into existence following the National Commission for Minorities Act 1992 brought by the Narasimha Rao-led United Front Government. The Act came into force on 17 May 1992. The debate on this Bill was opened by LK Advani who delivered a marathon speech opposing the Bill. Advani was candid enough to hold himself guilty for having been party to the creation of the Minorities Commission. He stated that the manifesto of the Janata Party did not commit itself to a Minorities Commission but only spoke of a Civil Rights Commission and claimed he was "hamstrung" while in government (Incidentally, the secularists can also claim to be hamstrung by the compulsions of power politics when they make demands and pass laws to appease minorities). Advani also raised some very valid objections to the proposed Act.

The official notification of the Act and the composition of the first seven-member statutory National Commission for Minorities were announced by two separate Government notifications issued on 17 May 1993.

In its manifesto for the 1998 general elections, the BJP had announced its intention to wind up the NCM and entrust its responsibilities to the National Human Rights Commission. After the NDA government came to power, some Opposition members asked Prime Minister Atal Behari Vajpayee in Parliament to state his government's policy about the NCM. The Prime Minister assured the members that there was no threat to the existence of the NCM. He was presumably hamstrung by the fact that the winding up of the NCM did not figure in the Common Minimum Programme of the NDA.

Various state-level minorities commissions are in place in different States. Andhra Pradesh, Bihar, Chhattisgarh, Delhi, Jharkhand, Karnataka, Madhya Pradesh, Rajasthan, Tamil Nadu, Uttar Pradesh, Uttarakhand and West Bengal are the twelve states that have made their state minorities commission a statutory body. The minority commissions in Maharashtra, Manipur and Punjab do not have a statutory status. Assam, Gujarat and Himachal Pradesh have non-statutory minorities boards. The setting up of state minorities commission is under process in the Andaman and Nicobar islands and Puducherry (Pondicherry) and under consideration in Kerala while a Bill towards the same has been passed by the Legislative Assembly in Tripura and submitted to the Union Ministry of Home Affairs for approval. The state of Haryana has specifically rejected the NCM demand to set up a state minority commission.

To the credit of the BJP, during 1995-1996, the Shiv Sena-BJP Government in Maharashtra and the BJP Government in Rajasthan had wound up the state minorities commissions in those states and a similar exercise was also undertaken in Uttar Pradesh in 1999. The case related to the Maharashtra State Minorities Commission, popularly called the Misbah Alam Case was heard by the Supreme Court. The state government stated that "it is the policy of the Government that all citizens are equal and there should not be any discrimination of minority-majority." The Supreme Court expressed its inability to issue a directive to the state government in this regard since there was no statute making it obligatory for the state government to reconstitute the Commission. It is worth bearing in mind that if the NCM were to be granted constitutional status in future, it will be obligatory for all state governments to constitute state minorities commissions without the option of dissolving them.

Mandate and Powers of the NCM

The definition of the word 'minority' is unclear in the NCM Act. As per the Act, the word 'minority' means "a community notified as such by the Central Government." It includes Muslims, Christians, Parsis, Sikhs and Buddhists.

A three judge bench of the Supreme Court consisting of Chief Justice R C Lahoti, Justice D M Dharmadhikari and Justice P K Balasubramanyan rejected the plea by the Jain community to the Supreme Court to advise the Central Government to notify it as a minority under Section 2 [C] of the NCM Act, 1992, in accordance with the recommendation of the NCM.[2] The judgment of that bench is worth quoting at some length. The learned bench observed: "The constitutional ideal, which can be gathered from the group of articles in the Constitution under Chapters of Fundamental Rights and Fundamental Duties, is to create social conditions where there remains no necessity to shield or protect rights of minority or majority.

"The above mentioned constitutional goal has to be kept in view by the Minorities Commissions set up at the Central or State levels. Commissions set up for minorities have to direct their activities to maintain integrity and unity of India by gradually eliminating the minority and majority classes. If, only on the basis of a different religious thought or less numerical strength or lack of health, wealth, education, power or social rights, a claim of a section of Indian society to the status of 'minority' is considered and conceded, there would be no end to such claims in a society as multi-religious and multi-linguistic as India is. A claim by one group of citizens would lead to a similar claim by another group of citizens and conflict and strife would ensure. As such, the Hindu society being based on caste, is itself divided into various minority groups. Each caste claims to be separate from the other. In a caste-ridden Indian society, no section or distinct group of people can claim to be in majority. All are minorities amongst Hindus. Many of them claim such status because of their small number and expect protection from the State on the ground that they are backward. If each minority group feels afraid of the other group, an atmosphere of mutual fear and distrust would be created posing serious threat to the integrity of our nation. That would sow seeds of multi-nationalism in India. It is, therefore, necessary that the Minority Commission should act in a manner so as to prevent generating feelings of multi-nationalism in various sections of people of Bharat."

An application by the petitioners to modify this order came before a three-Judge Bench with the Chief Justice of India on 9 July 2010 and the Honourable Chief Justice of India has referred it to a five-Judge Bench since "the matter involves issues of religious minority rights under the Constitution."

Various states such as Chattisgarh, Delhi, Jharkhand, Karnataka, Madhya Pradesh, Maharashtra, Uttar Pradesh, and Uttaranchal, have however notified Jains as a religious minority in accordance with their respective State Minority Commission Act. The Jain community has been declared as religious minority community in the State of Rajasthan for purpose of Article 30 and for no other purpose.

The NCM Act does not in effect include minorities like Jews and Bahais in its purview as these communities have not been notified as such. The Act does not extend to the State of Jammu and Kashmir.

Though the State has to be regarded as a unit for determining religious minority for the purpose of Article 30 of the Constitution, the Act does not deal with Hindus wherever they constitute a State-level minority as in five States and one Union Territory. To its credit, the NCM prepared a special 72-page report titled "NCM Actions and recommendations for the Hindus" in April 1999. The NCM performs all or any of the following functions, namely:

(a) evaluate the progress of the development of minorities under the Union and States.
(b) monitor the working of the safeguards provided in the Constitution and in laws enacted by Parliament and the State Legislatures.
(c) make recommendations for the effective implementation of safeguards for the protection of the interests of minorities by the Central Government or the State Governments.
(d) look into specific complaints regarding deprivation of rights and safeguards of the minorities and take up such matters with the appropriate authorities.
(e) cause studies to be undertaken on problems arising out of any discrimination against minorities and recommend measures for their removal.

(f) conduct studies, research and analysis on the issues relating to socio-economic and educational development of minorities.

(g) suggest appropriate measures in respect of any minority to be undertaken by the Central Government or the state governments.

(h) make periodical or special reports to the Central Government on any matter pertaining to minorities and in particular the difficulties confronted by them.

(I) any other matter which may be referred to it by the Central Government.

The NCM Act mandates that the Central Government shall cause the recommendations to be laid before each House of Parliament along with a memorandum explaining the action taken or proposed to be taken on the recommendations relating to the Union and the reasons for the non-acceptance, if any, of any of such recommendations. A similar action is to be taken where a State Government is concerned.

Importantly, the NCM has all the powers of a civil court including summoning and enforcing the attendance of any person from any part of India and examining him on oath, requiring the discovery and production of any document, receiving evidence of affidavits, requisitioning any public record or copy thereof from any court or office and issuing commissions for the examination of witnesses and documents, except when the matter is sub-judice. Such powers as are vested in the NCM are without parallel in any other part of the world. The US has no separate body that looks after religious minorities. The UK has institutions that concern themselves with racial minorities. However, the UK has stoutly resisted demands for setting up institutions dealing with religious minorities. The less said about the rights of religious minorities in communist havens like China the better. The religious minorities in India, specifically the Muslims, deny even the most basic rights to the non-Muslim minorities in countries where they form a majority. "When a minority, demand more and more rights in the name of democracy and minority rights and trample upon these values when in majority" is the watchword of Islam throughout history and worldwide.

The Political Role of the NCM

Being a statutory body, the NCM is supposed to be apolitical. There have been numerous occasions when the NCM and State Minorities Commissions have openly taken political stands. For example, in September 1997, a teenaged tribal boy had been repeatedly sodomized by a Christian priest in a Christian boys' hostel in Dumka, South Bihar. When protests, mainly by the enraged tribals, erupted in Dumka, the then chairman of the NCM Prof Tahir Mahmood blamed the protests on the sizeable BJP presence in Dumka. In December 1998, the NCM wrote to the Election Commission asking it to prevent the use of words like "vote-bank", "appeasement", "concessions" in reference to minorities in the forthcoming Lok Sabha elections. In July 1999, the NCM Chairman recommended individually to the heads of all major political parties that they should ensure adequate representation of the minorities in Parliament and all the state legislatures. He urged political parties to ensure at least 100 seats for minorities in the next Lok Sabha. In August 1999, Rev Dr James Massey, Member of the

NCM used government transport to attend a Press conference at St Savior's High School Meeting Hall, Ahmednagar, Maharashtra wherein the issue of the forthcoming Parliamentary and Assembly elections was discussed. He exhorted the Christian community to play a dynamic and important role in the forthcoming elections and asked the members of the church "to vote for such persons who will fight against Fascism, Brahminism and Manuvad and protect the poor, the Dalits and marginalised from such 'isms'." Such statements were made at the said press conference and pamphlets asking the Christian voters to desist from voting for BJP but instead vote for Congress and the Nationalist Congress Party were circulated. Dr Massey was arrested u/s 125 of the Representation of People's Act,1951, which deals with 'an attempt to promote on grounds of religion and community, feelings of hatred between different classes of the citizens of India.' In Tamil Nadu, crossing all limits of propriety, the Chairman of the State Minorities Commission who was a Christian missionary, actively campaigned for the local ruling party in the 1999 general elections.

Demands and Compliance

The NCM has been faithfully echoing the demands of powerful fundamentalist Islamic and Christian missionary lobbies. These demands are placed as 'recommendations' to the Central and State governments. Following is a list of some of the "recommendations" of the NCM (if complied with by the government, indicated in brackets):

1. Establishment of a Central Development and Finance Corporation for the Minorities (1991). (Formation of National Minori-

ties Development and Finance Corporation (NMDFC in 1994)

2. In 2003-04, the NCM recommended that school textbooks should be scrutinized to see whether there is any material that creates hatred for the minorities. (The New National Curriculum Framework 2005 addresses the concerns of the Commission and textbooks are being revised accordingly for several classes. The NCERT/CBSE has already introduced revised text books for Classes I, III, VI, IX and XI. NCERT sends the proposed new books in advance to NCM to enable its members to go through the portions pertaining to different religions)
3. There should be proportionate representation of minorities in the Armed Forces and Police. Officers belonging to minority communities should be given the so-called 'sensitive' assignments so that they can play a more useful role and also provide a "healing touch". (Central Para-Military Forces have been asked to ensure sufficient representation to minorities through making the minority community candidate aware of the employment opportunities and the incentives/prospects available in the Forces. Recruitment Boards have also been advised to send special information to the minority community run institutions/ organizations with a request to encourage candidates from these communities to apply for recruitment in Central Para-military forces. Further, the State Governments/UT Administrations have been advised that the state police forces should represent the social structure in their respective States so that the forces retain their secular character.)
4. Suitable steps should be taken to increase share of minority

communities in Public/private employment. (All public sector undertakings have been advised that wherever a Selection Committee/Board is constituted for making recruitment to 10 or more vacancies in Group 'C' and Group 'D' posts/services, it shall be mandatory to have one member belonging to a minority community in such committees/boards. Administrative Ministers have been requested to direct the officials in all public sector undertakings to ensure that interest of the minorities are taken care of. The Ministry of Railways, Government of India has already issued necessary instructions to all Indian Railways/PUs to ensure representation of minorities in Selection Committees/Boards.)

5. Adequate flow of credit to minority communities from nationalized banks for trade and business may be ensured. (All commercial banks, both in the public and private sector, have already been instructed by the Reserve Bank of India (RBI) to ensure smooth flow of credit to minority communities so that these communities could secure benefits flowing from various Government sponsored schemes. The RBI has also issued directions to banks specifically to promote financial inclusion. Further, the Reserve Bank also monitors the credit flow to minorities. Public sector banks have set state-wise targets for lending to minority communities as a percentage of Priority Sector Advances for the year 2009-10.)
6. The guidelines, regarding the preservation and management of enemy properties in India, vested in the Custodian of Enemy Property of India issued by CEP has no legal basis and should, therefore, be immediately withdrawn. The Custodian

of Enemy Property should ensure that no property notified as Wakf property under the relevant, statute is ever declared as Enemy Property. Action should be initiated to ensure that Wakf property is kept outside the purviews of the Enemy Property Act 1968. The Administration/CEP should not recover/demand any rent arrear of rent for a Property alleged to be an Enemy Property till such time as it is notified so under Section 12 of the Enemy Property Act, 1968. (The Enemy Property (Amendment and Validation) Bill is to be introduced in the Winter session of Parliament.)

7. On 27 October 2000, the NCM recommended to the Ministry of Law that while appointing Government Counsels, effort should be made to ensure that the members of the minority communities are adequately represented.
8. NCM made a statutory recommendation to UGC and Ministry of Human Resources Development for the grant of exemption to candidates belonging to minority communities from the requirement of clearing UGC's NET for 15 years for their appointment against teaching posts in all Colleges and Universities.
9. Draft bill of the Equal Opportunities Commission prepared by the NCM (Bill is under the process of inter-ministerial consultation; some ministers want the EOC to be limited for minorities only.)
10. Reservation for Dalit Christians and Muslims at par with SCs /STs should be considered by the government in all seriousness and all facilities extended.

A State Within a State

For some time now, the NCM is seeking constitutional status for itself. The pretext for seeking such an exalted status is familiar: "to inspire greater confidence among the minorities and to make the NCM effective in safeguarding their interests." The Constitution (one hundred and third amendment) Bill 2004 for granting Constitutional status to the NCM is pending since 2004. In order to give constitutional status to the NCM, the government had introduced the Constitution (One Hundred and Third Amendment) Bill 2004, and the NCM (Repeal) Bill, in the Lok Sabha. These were examined by the Parliamentary Standing Committee on Social Justice and Empowerment. Notices for official amendments and for consideration and passing of the Bills were sent to Lok Sabha in February 2009. However, the House was adjourned on 26 February 2009 and the Bill was not presented. With the dissolution of the 14th Lok Sabha, the Bills have lapsed.

The additional powers sought by the NCM are briefly given below:

(i) Investigate and monitor (instead of just monitor) the working of safeguards provided in the Constitution and the laws enacted by Parliament and the State Legislatures;

(ii) Inquire into specific complaints regarding deprivation of rights and safeguards of the minorities and to take up such matters with appropriate authorities.

(iii) Participate and advise in the planning process of socio-economic development of minorities and evaluate the progress of their development under the Union and any state.

Not content with its quasi-judicial nature (akin to a civil

court), the NCM has recommended insertion of a suitable provision to empower the Commission to take action under CrPC as and when its work as Civil Court is not responded to (for example, enforcing the direction of the Commission like summons, orders etc.)

The Way Ahead

The NCM has become a Frankenstein's monster out to undermine the Indian State in general and to disempower and emasculate the Hindus in particular. As a first step, Hindus have to be awakened to the draconian powers that the NCM will inevitably usurp if they fail to wake up to this looming danger. The secularist parties and specifically the Congress are committed to granting constitutional status to the NCM. A massive awareness and mobilization campaign needs to be launched against this proposed move and similar minority appeasement policies of Central and State governments. This needs to be done by the joint effort of Hindu organizations, various caste, sectarian and linguistic groups within the Hindu fold and like-minded non-Hindus. Parties such as the BJP that are perceived as Hindu nationalist should spell out their opposition in no uncertain terms. To begin with, the BJP governments in different states should scrap the state-level Minorities Commissions/Boards. This will trigger a debate on minority appeasement throughout the country. The BJP should stop putting forth the absurd proposition that "governance has no ideology" (When have you last heard a Laloo, Mayawati, Mani Shankar Aiyar or a Prakash Karat, not to speak of the Conservatives in the UK or the Republicans in the US mouthing such an inanity?). The BJP must stop using the alliance partners of the NDA as a fig-leaf for jettisoning Hindu interests, if it is to retain its political relevance.

In conclusion, I can do no better than once again quote Savarkar, "The Hindu Sanghatanists Party aims to base the future constitution of Hindusthan on the broad principle that all citizens should have equal rights and obligations irrespective of caste or creed, race or religion, provided they avow and owe an exclusive and devoted allegiance to the Hindusthani State. The fundamental rights of liberty of speech, liberty of conscience, of worship, of association etc. will be enjoyed by all citizens alike. Whatever restrictions will be imposed on them in the interest of the public peace and order of national emergency will not be based on any religious or racial considerations alone but on common national grounds....

> No Constitution, if it has to keep the integrity, sovereignty and strength of the National State safe, can go any further and that, it is all that is really required to safeguard any genuine special interests of the minorities as distinguished from those of the majority. Only that minority will insist to have still more and yet more to the last pound of flesh which in fact cherishes secret designs to disintegrate the State, to create a State within a State or altogether to subvert the National State and hold all others under its subjection.[3]

Most of the information given in the article is available in the various documents of the National Commission for Minorities as also online on its website www.ncm.nic.in. The book *Minorities Commission: Minor role in Major Affairs* by Tahir Mahmood, offers useful information. Muslim India, the monthly journal offers useful insight into Muslim thinking on strategic matters.

References

1. Government of India Resolution, Home Ministry Notification, No. II-160/2/2/77-NID.
2. Bal Patil Case; CA 4730 of 1999; 8 August 2005.
3. Presidential address to the Hindu Mahasabha, 21st session Calcutta 1939.

Appeasement Policy and the Kashmir Crisis

— T N Razdan

The word 'appease' which normally means to accede to demands, especially of an aggressor, has in modern times acquired political hues. Appeasement has become a political virus and compulsion, which is now gnawing at our national interest. It is an antibody that eats away the very subtle fibre of fraternity and integrity of the nation.

Unfortunately, this very appeasement has been the cornerstone of India's policy and attitude towards the region of Jammu & Kashmir, be it the appeasement of the Congress party towards Sheikh Mohammad Abdullah and his family in Kashmir, or increasingly now, of separatist elements and tendencies. As far as accountability for the Kashmir crisis is concerned, the Congress has perfected the art of simply passing the buck to everyone else.

It would be pertinent here to briefly delve into the historical background that nourished the separatist movement in Kashmir.

When Bharat the nation, was fighting for independence from the British rule, all forces from all corners, under any flag in the union or princely territories, affluent or oppressed buried their hatchet and united, to throw the European oppressor out, even though, unlike the earlier Islamic invaders and occupiers, he was not a forcible converter. The British too were intolerant of our Vedic heritage but they never resorted to mass slaughter, wanton destruction of temples or burning of our scriptures. For its part, the Indian nation never accepted the Mughals as its legitimate rulers and always considered them as aliens, who had forced themselves upon us.

The movement, for independence from the British, was led mainly by the Indian National Congress, though the revolutionary groups and many other outfits comprising of youth and thinkers too, were no less active.

In retrospect though, it appears evident that most national groups engaged in the struggle for independence from British rule, did not for a moment ponder on, what form of governance would replace the British rule. Gandhi's half-hearted and unimplemented slogan of "Ram Rajya" must be recognized for what it was—a slogan of no practical worth.

Unfortunately, the only identifiable group, who silently and shrewdly, overtly and covertly, conspired about what or who would follow the British, was that of the Muslims residing in India. We must today recognize the stark fact that Muslims had joined hands with Hindus in 1857—in the First War of Independence—not simply to oust the East India Company but reinstate Islamic rule over the country, i.e., over the Hindus. A detailed analysis of that defining event would be beyond the scope of this article.

The Indian National Congress never discussed or even questioned the first Partition of Bengal in 1905, in its 1905-06 'Bang Bhang resolution'. The Congress has always suppressed nationalist statement; Gandhi's support to the Khilafat Movement of 1916 is another atrocious example of appeasement. His conviction, that without keeping Muslims in good humour, independence could not be achieved, proved to be an exercise in self-delusion.

The Congress strictly followed Bapu's vision of the three monkeys when it came to dealing with neo pan-Islamic dreams. It utterly failed to glimpse any hint of a conspiracy even when the much heralded advocate-poet Mohammad wrote on 29 December, 1930: "I would like to see Punjab, NWFP Sindh and Baluchistan amalgamated into a single self-Government within British Empire or without British Empire at least NWFP". These very sentiments later on became the basis of what was articulated as the Two-Nation theory.

It was, therefore, no surprise when the Congress and especially Nehru later turned out to be so anti Maharaja (of J&K) and pro-Sheikh Abdullah. The Maharaja of J&K was the only ruler who whole-heartedly demanded an unconditional place of honour and equality for India in the Round Table Conference in London, (held from 12 November, 1930 to 19 January, 1931, quite against the wishes of the British, who expected him to toe the British line) an act of perfidy in their eyes, for which they never pardoned him. In fact, this writer would venture so far as to say that Sheikh Abdullah and Nehru worked in a combined manner for the avowed purpose of putting the Maharaja in his place. It is also a bitter fact that till 1942, the Indian National

Congress never wanted the British to quit entirely.

Upon his return, Maharaja Hari Singh faced trouble from the Muslims of Lahore who entered the state, inciting local Muslims against their ruler. Jathas of the Arhar Party from Punjab were pushed into the state. Another Lahore based body named Young Men's Muslim Association and their pamphlet *Inquilab* fanned Muslim communalism in Jammu province.

On 21 June 1931 widespread communal riots occurred in Srinagar and other places, in which Hindus lost their lives and property. When the Maharaja arrested the culprit, a Qadiyani Muslim called Qadeer, a Muslim mob attacked the prison where he was lodged, on 13 July 1931. When this attempt was aborted by the Maharaja's guards, Kashmiri Pandits became the soft target, and were attacked and killed, their properties looted and houses burnt. Kashmir witnessed another revival of Muslim onslaught after Afghan rule. In fact, Henry Lawrence wrote (about the Maharaja's administration): "It is difficult to realise that change has come over Kashmir in the short period of Dogra rule—a period of less than 50 years. Anarchy and constant warfare has been succeeded by complete peace."

In Kashmir the British resident had already started grooming a Qadiyani follower, Sheikh Mohammad Abdullah, to revolt against the Hindu Maharaja. In October 1932, Sheikh Abdullah constituted the All J&K Muslim Conference with the avowed purpose of dislodging the Hindu king. Clearly, the Muslim majority in the state would not tolerate a Hindu ruler. The name of the Muslim Conference was changed to National Conference at the instance of communist politicians, who were more intent than

Muslims on dislodging Maharaja Hari Singh. The unambiguous slogan was "No Hindu ruler in Muslim-dominated state". And to think that the top icon of the Congress, Nehru, made such a man his "best friend"! That wasn't all, though. The then Congress President Maulana Abdul Kalam Azad, Nehru and Abdul Samadh Khan addressed a conference, thus lending legitimacy to a Muslim uprising against the king.

One wonders how Nehru could give such a seditious speech against the ruler of a state and read out sermons to non-Muslims, on a matter in which he had no locus standi. The extent of Congress and Nehruvian appeasement of the Kashmir Valley's rabid separatist Muslims can be gauged from a rabble-rousing speech of Jawaharlal Nehru during the first week of August 1945, quoted by D N Raina: "If Kashmiri Pandits want to live in Kashmir they should join the National Conference or else should bid goodbye to the state. National Conference is the real organization. If the Pandits do not join it, no safeguards and weightages can protect them. There is no alternative for them except to join National Conference." Not surprisingly, emboldened by this speech of Nehru, the Sheikh and his followers echoed everywhere: "*Bataw ralive chalive ya galive*" "Pandits! Either mix, run away or perish". Nehru doubled the miseries of the Maharaja Hari Singh when he allowed the Sheikh to visit him in Delhi, Lahore and elsewhere to rejuvenate the engineered unrest against the king.

In 1946, Sheikh Abdullah gave a highly inflammatory speech inciting people for "direct action and revolt" against the king. After delivering the speech, however, he ran for shelter to Punjab but Maharaja Hari Singh arrested him for treason, at the Kohala check-post. Nehru impetuously jumped into an agitation against the arrest, though he had absolutely no *locus standi* whatsoever to do so. Sheikh Abdullah, who was prevented from entering the state, invited Pakhtoon goons to attack state forces, as result of which he was arrested on 19 June 1946 at Kohala and detained in the state Dak Bungalow. Nehru said "Srinagar is a city of the dead," whereas the fact, which is on record, is that not even a simple lathi charge took place that day. Acharya Kriplani, then president of the Congress, ridiculed this act of Nehru, but the damage had been done.

Sheikh Abdullah, knowing that he would suffer severe punishment for treason, pleaded for mercy and escaped with three years' imprisonment. The Congress stalwart Nehru, who had jumped into an agitation without any approval from his party, to seek the release of Sheikh Abdullah, had also violated the state laws of Maharaja Hari Singh, which forbade entry without permission. Nehru incited Pakhtoon warlords to attack the state administration.

Accession

A serious question of national importance arises as to how Nehru, in September 1947, could persuade Sardar Patel to ask the Maharaja of J&K to release his culprit (Sheikh Abdullah) and negotiate the future course of action with him? Why did Nehru not ask Patel straightway to seek accession then and there? Why did he seek the release of his friend before he could think of accession? Accession was the prerogative of Maharaja Hari Singh, after all.

Was Sheikh Abdullah so popular a leader, of the whole state

of J&K that he could not be dispensed with? The answer is a resounding No. He was never accepted, not even received by the Muslim populace of Mirpur, Kotli or Muzaffarabad. There is no record to show that Sheikh ever visited Gilgit, Dras or Skardu. He did not even know what the territory of Ladakh was like. He was never accepted by Jammuites. The limit of his influence was the Vale of Kashmir, more particularly from Qazigund to Uri.

The bare truth is that Sheikh Abdullah's only qualification was that of a stooge of the British, deployed through the Qadiyani sect of Muslims to seek revenge against Maharaja Hari Singh for his nationalist stand at the Second Round Table Conference in London. The Qadiyani sect has never been accepted by general Muslims as Muslim, anywhere. They hate the Qadiyani sect, for the latter do not accept the Mohammad as the Last Messenger or Prophet of Allah.

Because of Nehru's intervention, the King, under his plenary powers, granted clemency to the Sheikh by remitting his remaining period of conviction. He was released on 29 September 1947 and paid *Nazrana* to the King as a token of loyalty. But blinded by the syndrome of appeasement, Nehru, in less than a week after the Sheikh's release from jail, sent a cherished, intelligent comrade G M Sadiq to negotiate with Pakistani leaders in Lahore. Micheal Brecher confirms in this regard: "Early in October, a delegation of National Conference went to Pakistan in an unsuccessful endeavour to gain support for the policy of freedom before accession."[39]

On 5 October, the same Sheikh who had paid *Nazrana* to the King soon after his release on 29 September 1947 addressed a gathering in Srinagar and thundered: "Our first demand is complete transfer of power to the people in Kashmir. Representatives of the people in the democratic Kashmir will then decide whether the state should join India or Pakistan. If forty lakhs of people living in Jammu and Kashmir are by-passed and the state declares its accession to India or Pakistan, I shall raise the banner of revolt and we will face struggle."

Pakistan, understanding the Sheikh's lust for power and Nehru's abettment, besides the King's dilemma, armed the ungovernable wild communities of its North West Frontier Province particularly Mahsuds, Wazirs, Swatis, Afridis and Burnerwal tribes. In all, it pushed 60,000 Pathans into the state under the command of Pak Army Major General Akbar Khan nicknamed General Tariq. In this hour of crisis, Sheikh Abdullah abandoned the Valley and sought refuge in Nehru's home at Delhi.

Maharaja Hari Singh, who was the absolute monarch (because of the powers given to him by Section Six of the Government of India Act 1935 and the Indian Independence Act of 1947, passed by British Parliament) acceded 222, 236 kilometers of territory by way of the Instrument of Accession to the Domain of India, despite the fact that the domain was headed by Governor General Lord Mountbatten and Prime Minister Jawaharlal Nehru.

The question is: how could Nehru, a barrister and a so-called intellectual, without calling a Cabinet meeting, refuse the Document of Accession drafted by a king within the ambit of law? Mehar Chand Mahajan, the then secretary to the Prime Minister, records: 'I met the Prime Minister and Deputy Prime Minister for India and apprised them of the serious and dangerous situation in the State. I solicited Army help and said that the Army must be flown at once, otherwise the whole town of Srinagar and all we hold valuable would be completely destroyed. I was asked how an army could be sent at a moment's notice. I took the firm stand: "give the Army, take accession and give whatever power you want to the popular party but the Army must fly to Srinagar this evening otherwise I will go and negotiate terms with Jinnah, as the city must be saved." At this Nehru flew into a rage and told me to get out. Just as I was getting up, Sheikh Abdullah (who was staying in the Prime Minister's house and overheared the talks) sensing a critical situation, sent a slip of paper to the Prime Minister who read it and said that what I was saying was also the view of Sheikh Sahib. His attitude had changed completely.'

The total area under the rule of Maharaja Hari Singh was 222,236 sq km. Maharaja Hari Singh was forced to lease the civil and military administration of Gilgit to the British for 60 years on 26.3.1935. But on pretext of personal difficulty, in February 1947 the British wanted the lease to terminate not later than June 1947, for obvious political reasons. Brigadier Ghansar Singh took over as Governor of Gilgit from the British political agent Lt Col Bacon on 1 August 1947. Out of 222,236 kilometers, 78,114 kilometers are under the illegal occupation of Pakistan called PoK, left un-liberated in 1947. China usurped 37,555 km in Ladakh in the 1962 war. Out of 78,114 kilometers, Pakistan illegally handed over 5,180 kilometers to China vide the Sino-Pakistan Treaty of 1963. The state is almost a mountainous region with a strip of level land along the borders of Punjab, now in Pakistan.

The Congress has been no more than a mute spectator or worse, a tacit consenter to all the malevolent acts of Nehru. Can any sane person with even ordinary intelligence or morals, accept the fact that a legitimate ruler was asked to step down in favour of a convicted prisoner? Maharaja Hari Singh's only crime was that he cared for his subjects and wanted to join the Indian nation.

After Maharaja Hari Singh vacated the state, under most reprehensible and uncalled for, illegitimate and immoral dictates and pressure, Nehru started grooming the Sheikh. In 1949, he accepted the Sheikh's demand of introducing Article 370 in the Constitution of India, against the wishes and objections of the entire Constituent Assembly. Nehru virtually begged N Gopalaswamy Iyenger to introduce the Article in his absence. He refused to treat J&K on par with other Indian states. To please the Sheikh he was prepared to dilute the mandate of three declared charters stated in the Instrument of Accession, i.e., Defence Communication and External Affairs. In 1950, the Sheikh enacted the draconian law of big landed estates Abolition Act. By this Act, he abolished the landholders' right to land and passed it on to the tillers, free of any cost or compensation. This act was so drafted and implemented that every royal associate of the former king was forced into penury. Nehru patted the Sheikh for this so-called "socialist" act. After the results of the complete implementation of this act became evident, Nehru had to cut a sorry figure. This draconian Act could not be challenged as fundamental rights were not granted to J&K's subjects and the Supreme Court had no jurisdiction.

In 1952, Nehru, in defiance of the cabinet and party, unilaterally entered into an agreement with the Sheikh known as Delhi Declaration. How could one single individual consider himself above the laws of the nation to please his friend at the cost of law and national interests? The Congress is answerable for this.

Nehru agreed to the Sheikh hoisting his state flag alongside the national flag. He permitted him to have his own constitution. He permitted him to choose his own *Sadar-e-Riyasat*, i.e., President of the State. The Sheikh rigged the very first election in which 75 members were elected unopposed. Elections after that have been rigged. When the Praja Prashad started a satyagraha against these acts, the movement was crushed by the Sheikh's regime, with peaceful demonstrators being gunned down. The moveable properties of the demonstrators were confiscated. When a delegation of nationalist people came to seek intervention from Nehru, he refused to meet them and dubbed the delegation itself as "communal". He encouraged his friend and "Prime Minister of the State" to let loose a reign of terror on the whole of Jammu province. Sheikh Abdullah acted on this Nehruvian command and treated the Hindus of Jammu as "pro-Maharaja subjects".

It is amply clear that Nehru never listened to his party or to the warnings of Dr Shyma Prasad Mukherji. His letters on record show his idiosyncratic attitude. He blindly believed Sheikh Abdullah on all matters relating to the sensitive and nationally strategic region of Jammu & Kashmir.

The Congress for its part, blindly supported Nehru in his blind appeasement of Islamic separatism. They encouraged the Sheikh to go ahead with his policy of 'power to the people of J&K'. Encouraged by the Congress, Sheikh Abdullah even began hobnobbing with the US to seek complete independence from India. In fact, final talks to declare an 'independent Kashmir' had begun in Gulmarg. Intelligence reports alarmed Nehru, who under severe pressure from sane and nationlist-minded cabinet members spoke to Bakshi Ghulam Mohammad, the Deputy Prime Minister, and *Sadar-e-Riyast* Dr Karan Singh and then was forced to dismiss Sheikh from his "prime ministership". Nehru favoured his friend's dismissal but not his arrest. However, Sheikh Abdullah had to be arrested on 9 August 1953.

Even after his release in 1958, Sheikh Abdullah did not change his attitude. In February 1965, he requested permission to proceed on a Haj pilgrimage, to which New Delhi agreed. But after completing his Haj, Sheikh Abdullah visited Muslim countries to seek their intervention, to put pressure on India to agree to an independent J&K state. Abdullah also visited Pakistan and during the middle of March 1965, he also had a meeting with Chinese Prime Minister Chou En Lai. Since diplomatic relations with China had been snapped in that period, the Sheikh's passport was cancelled and on arrival at Delhi airport he was detained and sent to Utakamandal.

Pakistani dictator Gen Auyb Khan's grand design of snatching Kashmir failed miserably in the 1965 war, as India's then Prime Minister took Gen Chaudhury into confidence and permitted him to teach Pakistan a lesson. Pakistan lost the Sialkot train junction and the Ichogil bridge was destroyed by India, breaking the neck of the Pakistani supply route. The Tashkent Agreement between a victorious India and the defeated Pakistan was virtually a sell-out of the country's strategic interests, forced by the intervention of USSR. The restoration of the status quo meant that precious territory gained by sacrifices of Indian soldiers was retuned under dubious international agreements. A sensitive Lal Bahadur

Shastri lost his life. 1971, Pakistan was comprehensively defeated and Bangladesh was liberated by our armed forces, but the then prime minister Indira Gandhi let off 90,000 Pakistani prisoners of war. She returned strategically important conquered peaks in Poonch, Mendhar, Lam Jourian and above all Chamb, a highly fertile patch of land. Sheikh Abdullah, finding Pakistan a wreck and of no use to him, began courting Indira, Nehru's daughter and not surprisingly succeeded. The ancient Chankya's political wisdom "one who betrays once can betray again" was ignored. The Indira-Sheikh Abdullah Accord came into being. Indira proved that she was after all Nehru's daughter when it came to betraying the country's long-term interests.

The sordid tale has continued throughout India's history. After Sheikh Abdullah's death in September 1983, Indira Gandhi installed his son Dr Farooq Abdullah against the wishes of MLAs of NC as they favoured Gul Shah. After Indira Gandhi's assassination in 1984, the Congress supported Gul Shah in order to remain in power but he proved even more communal than his predecessor. A room of the Bhua Dita Temple in the Secretariat was converted into a mosque, creating unrest in Jammu. In February 1986, the locks of the Ram Temple at Ayodhya were opened and in retaliation, more than 100 temples in the state were soiled with filth, broken and torched. Farooq and Mufti Mohammad Sayeed joined hands in looting and breaking every Hindu house in Anantnag and surrounding villages, while Baramulla witnessed open clashes, with the Srinagar regime remaining indifferent.

Indira's son Rajiv who had been hurriedly made the country's Prime Minister following her assassination, first called Farooq "anti-national" and then went on to sign an accord with him and contest elections in March 1987 on one platform. In Srinagar, televisions relayed the news of the accord and broadcast a joint statement of the two leaders on Srinagar TV. Farooq Abdullah said, "I am a Muslim and Rajiv a Hindu and we will put up a joint fight." Rajiv promptly said, "I am not a Hindu." Though soon after, around 8 pm, Doordarshan Delhi while relaying news of this joint rally, cut out Rajiv Gandhi's statement wherein he had uttered the words "I am not a Hindu". The true colours of Congress appeasement of Muslim separatism could not have been more apparent.

In November 1989, after Islamic terrorism, sponsored, aided and abetted by Pakistan, began to terrorise and kill Kashmir's Hindu population, Farooq Abdullah ran away from the state. He did not remain in India but took shelter in England. How and why? Nobody asked. Kashmiri Pandits were threatened and then brutally killed, and unspeakable atrocities were committed on Kashmiri Hindu women. This has been one of the biggest tales of genocide in human history. It is the Congress policy of appeasement, of violent, separatist and expansionist Islamic zealotry and the criminal disregard for the nation, its safety and its long-term future that has brought about this sorry state of affairs.

Pan-Islam and its Effects on Kashmir

The Pan-Islamic movement and its fallout in Kashmir has been worse than anywhere in North India, because the Valley has no connectivity from its Pir Panjal range with the rest of India.

When Mohammad bin Qasim invaded Sindh and was successful because of his treacherous war tactics, Prince Jai Singh, son of the defeated and slain King Dahir, took shelter in Kashmir and was presented an estate by the then King of Kashmir. Unfortunately, Jai Singh was accompanied by a Muslim, Syrian friend Hamid, who became the first Muslim to enter the Valley. After the death of Jai Singh, Hamid took the charge of the estate and started propagating Islam. Unnoticed by the King, he established a foothold for Islamic invaders against the rulers. The follies of King Harsha and conspiracy of Bulbul Shah Darvesh and Shamiri converted Rinchan, a fugitive of Tibet, who had taken shelter under King Sahdev of Kashmir, to Islam. During the rule of Sahdev, because of the conspiracies of Bulbul Shah and Shamiri, a horde of Sayyeds from Turkey and Persia poured in, following the onslaught of Taimur upon India. Later, the Mughals during Aurangzeb's rule, spared no atrocities on native Hindus of Kashmir.

The takeover by Afghans from the Mughals is the darkest era in Kashmir, full of forcible conversions. Thousands of Brahmins preferred drowning in the Dal Lake than eating beef. Brahmins' sacred threads were burnt by Sikandar Butshiken.

It was in 1756 that some Kashmir nobles approached Maharaja Ranjit Singh for help. Sikh rulers put an end to Afghan rule and one can vouchsafe that from the advent of Sikh Rule succeeded by the Dogras. From 1856 till 1947, Kashmir did not witness any religious persecution oppression or imposition of the hated Jaziya tax.

Freedom at Midnight may have brought some respite to the rest of India but brought total dismay to Jammu & Kashmir. It is the Congress Party headed by "secularists" like Maulana Azad and its leaders, Gandhi and Nehru, which is squarely responsible for the present crises that still continues to bleed Mother India.

The Partition of India is a tragedy, for which Mohammad Ali Jinnah can never be forgiven. For this inhuman tragedy, the Indian National Congress cannot be forgiven, either. This writer would like to quote what Clement Attlee (former Prime Minister of Britain in 1947) said...

"The Leaders of Indian National Congress had in all reality made the majority of Indian nation, follow Gandhi's three monkeys and not look at the treacherous deeds of Muslim League and the Muslim Ulema. They did not hear the anguished cries of Bengal during the Bang Bhang and did not take note of 1942 events monitored by Iqbal. They did not raise their voice against British-Muslim ties."

The British, in the pursuit of their interests, wanted to keep an eye on (the then) USSR and wanted the area of Gilgit to be kept under their own control to which Maharaja Hari Singh did not agree. The King was compelled to lease Gilgit to British for sixty years and the region was under a lease agreement with the British till 1970.

The treachery of the Muslim League was ignored by the Congress which maintained a silence, just as it did, when the sovereign territory of Tibet was annihilated by China in 1954. The Congress could only pay lip service to the empty slogans of Panchsheel and *Hindi Chini Bhai Bhai*. The nation had to pay the price for the Congress perfidy in 1962.

Kashmir is the worst sufferer of Congress policies. A portion of the state continues to remain under the illegal occupation of the Chinese.

UPA's Appeasement of Minorities Debilitating and Dangerous

— Vinod Shukla

My present paper shall restrict itself to the objective analysis of the minority appeasement. There is a pressing need of dispassionate analysis of the issue, as the matter concerns not only individuals, but the whole country as such. As journalists, we are witness to many events and developments and tend to get detached from them while reporting them. My effort would be to do justice to the subject, as it is indeed a very serious matter, one that becomes more serious when we talk about the financial aspects of minority appeasement. When we talk about this particular aspect, we must not forget that resources in the country are limited and thus valuable.

The government must ensure equitable distribution of resources considering the social structure of the country. But politicians in our country have the habit of getting carried away and going overboard for grabbing political mileage. An example of this was provided some time back, when Prime Minister Manmohan Singh declared that "Muslims have the first right over the resources of the country." Why did the government (read PM) suddenly remember the need to uplift the condition of Muslims only? What about the other minorities and the weaker sections of the society? Several questions ought to be posed to the Prime Minister but two basic questions cannot be ignored:

First, an observation of this nature from a Prime Minister of a county, supposedly committed to secularism, that only Muslims have the first right over the country's resources, smacks of a rank attempt at communal pandering. One would be right in asking: does the government desire the welfare of minorities at all? Second, the "secular" PM has not bothered to explain thereafter, why only Muslims have the first right over the resources of the country. Is not the Prime Minister's declaration tantamount to endorsing a "special status for Muslims? Do other minority communities have to wait for their claims over national resources only after the Muslim community is satisfied? Is the government done with welfare and uplift of Dalits, farmers, labourers and Other Backward Classes (OBCs), who have been suffering since ages?

There is little need to ponder or look far for an answer to this question. Evidently, Manmohan Singh and his colleagues are aiming at their favourite vote-bank. There are several organs of the government, which can announce schemes specific to socio-economic segments, but why is the head of the government so vocal in his preference for a particular community—in this case the Muslims—serious questions have to be asked.

Why have a separate ministry for minority affairs, when

issues pertaining to minorities are taken up by other ministries? Isn't it a blatant attempt to tell Muslims that the government is more 'concerned' about their welfare, at the exclusion of others? It is difficult to miss the communal punch-line, camouflaged in the prime minister's missive—the UPA regime is ready to pander to every whim of the community but it has to keep backing the regime, especially in terms of precious votes.

Even a cursory look at the policies, programmes and expenditure of the UPA coalition would make it clear, prima facie, that it spares no attempt to keep the Muslim community happy, especially as their voting pattern can make a difference in many regions of the country. It is also difficult to buy the argument that the government is unaware of the alienation caused by such initiatives. Nor can it be unaware about the divisiveness caused by such initiatives, which also breed divisive anti-national politics of a competitive nature. Tragically, the ruling regime continues to indulge in Ostrich-like behavior. The dangers of such a tendency can hardly be exaggerated.

A separate Minority Affairs Ministry was constituted despite the fact that most issues related to minorities fall under the purview of other ministries. Besides that, a glance at year-wise plan allocations, expenditure and percentage utilization is sufficient to reveal the intentions of the government—its spending is anything but result-oriented. In the year 2007-08, its estimated budget for 'minorities' was Rs 500 crore, which has gone up to Rs 2,600 crore by 2010-11. More notably, this particular budgetary expenditure was 39.33 per cent in 2007-08 but sky-rocketed to 98.33 per cent in 2009, an election year! The UPA's intention is clear—it is not development that motivates its appeasement of the Muslim community, with election years being a premium time for handouts.[1]

Doling out scholarships and salaries to *mufties* are part of the UPA's new handout exercises, evident from its schemes launched by the Ministry of Minority Affairs in 2009-10. The Ministry provided 756 fellowships for research scholars from minority communities under the Maulana Azad National Fellowship Scheme, sanctioned for pursuing MPhil and PhD.

The UPA regime is also excessively worked up about Waqf properties, apart from being ultra-eager in opening new campuses of Aligarh Muslim University and Jamia Milia Islamia in minority-dominated districts. This will doubtlessly encourage divisive tendencies in the bargain. For the record, computerization of records of Waqf Boards: software development and strengthening of State Waqf Boards (SWBs) for implementation of this scheme are in progress. Strengthening of Central Waqf Council is another of the UPA's sops to the Muslims. Around 171 National Level Monitors (NLMs) have been empanelled, trained and deployed for monitoring implementation of various schemes of the Ministry.

The objective appears to be to spend as much money of the nation's taxpayers as possible, in order to entice Muslim votes. Under the Prime Minister's new 15-Point Programme for the Welfare of Minorities, the Ministry has introduced three scholarship schemes detailed below. Since 2007-08, 29.39 lakh scholarships have been awarded to the students from minority communities. Pre-matric scholarships were launched in 2008-09 with a target of three lakh scholarships with an allocation of Rs 79 crore, which have gone up to 20 lakh and Rs 450 crore, respectively. Similar is the case with the post-matric scholarship target, which was 75,000 students in 2007-08, the year it was launched, with a fund allocation of Rs 60 crore that was enhanced to 4 lakh and Rs 265 crore respectively. A merit-cum-means scholarship scheme for technical and professional courses was launched in 2007-08 and 79,435 scholarships have been awarded cumulatively.

Another Meritorious Girl's Scholarship Scheme of the Maulana Azad Education Foundation (MAEF) has cumulatively awarded 34,991 scholarships to meritorious girl students since 2006-07. Under the PM's new 15-Point Programme, in such schemes 15 per cent of targets were fixed for minorities, with 4,457 primary and upper primary schools and 20,588 additional class rooms constructed, 3,530 new primary and upper primary schools opened, 7,765 teachers and 27 KGBVs sanctioned under the Sarva Shiksha Abhiyan in 2009-10.

Since 2008-09, around 6,749 additional class rooms, 559 school buildings and eight hostels have been approved and 105 additional class rooms, 215 school buildings and 62 hostels have been approved in-principle under Multi-sectoral Development Programme (MsDP) for Minority Concentration Districts (MCDs). Equitable Share in Economic Activities and Employment, with the objective of ensuring equitable share to minorities in economic activities and employment is sought to be achieved through these schemes and programmes. The approach of the government should have been development of people across society and religion, which unfortunately is not there in this case.

The National Minorities Development and Finance

Corporation (NMDFC) is also active in providing loans to the minorities. However, the very formation of the NMDFC was opposed by a former Muslim cabinet member of the former V P Singh government when it was being discussed in the cabinet. The minister argued that this move would not help the community but only alienate them further and cause a divide in society at large. The minister argued that the Muslim community would face more problems in obtaining loans from other financial institutions as they have a separate financial institution for the community. He argued that an administrative matter, in which the government was unable to facilitate loans to Muslims easily, has been given a religious colour. Cumulatively, Rs 585.35 crore of term loans and micro finance have been disbursed to 2.51 lakh beneficiaries since 2006-07. Rs 197.74 crore were disbursed to 1.045 lakh beneficiaries in 2009-10. Around 1,759 bank branches have been opened in districts having a substantial minority population since 2007-08. During 2009-10, around 699 bank branches were opened. Priority Sector Lending (PSL) for minorities, which stood at Rs 58,662.67 crore in 2007-08, has increased to Rs 1,08,850.89 crore in 2009-10. This represents 9.67 per cent of the total PSL in 2007-08 and 12.64 per cent in 2009-10. The target for minorities for the next three years has been fixed at 15 per cent of total PSL.

The government also has schemes like free coaching for minority students and other allied schemes. The scheme was revised and launched in 2006-07 and a cumulative total of more than 15,000 students/candidates have benefited. 5,532 persons were covered under this scheme during 2009-10, with the target for 2010-11 being 5,760. The recruitment of persons from minority communities in ministries, public sector undertakings, public sector banks and financial institutions, railways etc has increased from 12,182 in 2006-07 to 15,172 in 2008-09, representing 6.92 per cent of the total recruitment in 2006-07 and 9.24 per cent in 2008-09. However, the actual numbers are bigger than this.

There are plans for infrastructure building for skilled education exclusively for Muslims. Eight ITIs have been approved and 47 have been approved in-principle for construction and upgrading in the minority concentration districts under MSDP. Besides, eight new polytechnics have been approved in-principle for construction in minority concentration districts. Under the new 15-Point Programme, 60 existing ITIs are being upgraded into Centres of Excellence.

The government is providing houses to minority families under the PM's 15 Point Programme, 5.43 lakh minority families have benefited from Indira Awas Yojna (IAY) houses at a total cost of Rs 1459.69 crore in 2009-10. Under MSDP, 2.19 lakh IAY houses have been sanctioned in MCDs at a cost of Rs 639.59 crore. Out of 2,37,453 habitations, 1,70,629 habitations having substantial minority population have been covered under National Rural Drinking Water Programme. Under MSDP, 26,686 units of drinking water supply facilities have been sanctioned in MCDs at a cost of Rs 145.18 crore. Access to health and facilities for women and child development: Under the PM's new 15 Point Programme, 23,712 anganwadi centres have been operationalized in blocks having a substantial minority concentration in 2009-10.

Of course, no one can object to Muslims availing of facilities from the government. But the policy of the government in disbursing benefits because of their religion is a gross violation of India's Constitution, which does not permit reservations based on religion. Moreover, this is a government that is scarcely bothered about the plight of Dalits and poor farmers, particularly in regions like Vidharba in Maharashtra and Bundelkhand in Uttar Pradesh, where the maximum numbers of famers' suicides are taking place. Practically the entire rural Bundelkand has been forced to migrate to cities, with several villages registering migration of up to 90 per cent. The region does not have infrastructure for industry nor proper facilities for agriculture.

In the name of strengthening of institutions, the Waqf (Amendment) Bill, 2010 was passed in the Lok Sabha on 7 May 2010. Financial assistance has been released to 11 State Waqf Boards and Central Waqf Council. The National Informatics Centre (NIC) has been commissioned to develop software modules for Waqf boards. A scheme has been approved for strengthening of Central Waqf Council and one for strengthening of State Waqf Boards is under formulation. All this largesse is for an institution that is self-sufficient as far as resources are concerned. According to the Sachchar Commission the total worth of Waqf properties in the country is around Rs 1.25 lakh crore. Yet, the UPA government wants to "rehabilitate" it. On the other hand, the "secular" regime's attitude towards institutions of other religions is known to all.

Several other moves to woo Muslims are still in process. The proposal for setting up the Equal Opportunity Commission (EOC) was sent to the Cabinet on 13 October 2010. However, this proposal, which is currently under the consideration of a Group of Ministers (GOM), was opposed by many civil rights groups and the move was halted, at least for the time being. The Assessment and Monitoring Authority (AMA) and National Data Bank (NDB) have already been set up. The report of the National Commission for Religious and Linguistic Minorities (NCRLM), which is better known as the Ranganath Mishra Commission, is under consideration as well. Several minority leaders have admitted that almost 24 recommendations have been accepted by the UPA government.

The government has earmarked 90 minority concentrated districts and a special area development programme known as the Multi-Sectoral Development Programme (MSDP) is being implemented from 2008-09. The Cabinet had approved an allocation of Rs 3,780 crore for the MsDP, but the Planning Commission had reduced it to Rs 2,750 crore in the 11th Five Year Plan. However, the ministry is implementing the schemes approved by the Cabinet without any regard to financial constraints when it comes to minority appeasement. The total amount released to the States under the programme is Rs 1,243.87 crore and expenditure reported by the States/UTs is Rs 253.27 crore, which is 20.36 per cent of the releases made. Implementation on the ground started only after the last general elections in May 2009. Under the programme, district plans of 80 districts have been approved, of which 15 MCD plans have been fully approved and 65 district plans have been partially approved. District plans of nine MCDs (seven in Arunachal Pradesh and two in Assam) are still awaited.

Former Chief Minister of Andhra Pradesh (now deceased)

Y S Rajashekhar Reddy had decided on waiving fees of Muslim students in graduate courses such as engineering, medical and law, which is extremely dangerous and will not stand scrutiny in any court of law. This decision is a typical example of how students of the majority community are gradually becoming victims of minority appeasement. This is not only creating a sense of discomfort among poor students but it also violates the very basis of giving equal footing to the poor Hindu students. Students in colleges can see that their fellow students do not have to pay fees simply because they are Muslims, while no matter what their financial position is they have to pay the full fees. The fee-waiver scheme should be on the basis of economic and not religious criteria. The government's spending of such enormous sums of money on a scheme is a clear pursuit of its vote-bank politics, a grave threat to the nation.

The Centre moots spending more than Rs 3,500 crore in infrastructure development projects in 90 minority-dominated districts across the country, following its approval of a package for improving basic amenities in these areas. Just before the tenure of the UPA I government ended, it announced the major Multi-Sectoral Development Programme, under which basic infrastructure projects were to be undertaken during the 11th Plan in designated districts. The Centre would bear the entire expense of Rs 3,780 crore while the local governments would help in implementation of projects. Under the scheme, basic infrastructure like roads, health centres, skill development centres and marketing facilities would be developed in the minority-dominated districts.

The government official said the focus of the scheme will

be on rural and semi-rural areas of the identified 90 minority concentration districts which will be given funds as development deficits. The money will be given after seeking a commitment from the state governments that they will constitute a committee for implementation of the Prime Minister's 15-point programme for the welfare of minorities. The PM's 15-point programme also talks about modernizing madrassa. The question is: why is a constitutionally mandated "secular" government providing money to madrassas? The government has no dearth of funds to invest in building schools and colleges, which will provide good education and mould the children to serve the country.

The UPA government has also come out with 20,000 scholarships every year for minorities. These scholarships are to be given for higher studies above 12th standard HSC level. What is the requirement of merit for these scholarships? A mere 50 per cent marks in HSC examinations! Are we to believe that those candidates whose parents receive up to Rs 20,000 a month are in such dire monetary need of these scholarships? What is the greatest "qualification" of these candidates? They are from the minority community! The Constitution of India declares that no citizen of India shall be discriminated on grounds of his or her religion. But let us take a close look at what is happening now. Indeed, one must examine what has been happening in the last 60 years or so.

Muslim and Christian-dominated states in the country are receiving 3.6 times more funds than relatively poorer states, from the central government in terms of per capita expenditure. In the north eastern region, Christian-dominated states receive three times more funding than Hindu states in terms of per capita central assistance.

The people of Jammu and Kashmir get 3.5 times more central funds in terms of per capita assistance. The ratio of BPL people in Bihar is 41 per cent against the BPL ratio of mere five per cent in Jammu and Kashmir. Even within J&K, the lion's share of central aid is appropriated by the Valley, which is dominated by Muslims, while Hindu-dominated Jammu and predominantly Buddhist Ladakh continue to suffer step-motherly treatment.

Central allocation to Muslim dominated states is more than any other states. There is gross discrimination as far as per capita central allocation is concerned. India is the only country where majority-dominated states are facing jihadi terrorist threat, but the government has meekly surrendered to them. States like Jammu & Kashmir are reeling under Islamic terrorism and ethnic cleansing of Kashmiri Hindus. The Kashmiri Pandit community, which was forced to leave the Valley, live as pitiable refugees in tents in Delhi but Bhagalpur riot victims are getting a pension of Rs 2,500 per month. Is this our democratic equality?

The Congress has spared no effort to please its Muslim vote-bank. At macro-level, the Congress has constituted the Minority Commission and another commission, specifically to deal with minorities' education.[2] It has constituted three Muslim universities —Rafi Ahmed Kidwai University in Murshidabad, the Tipu Sultan University in Karnataka and the Khwaja Moinuddin Chisti University in Ajmer. The UPA regime has also sanctioned Rs 70,000 crore for 'uplift' of the community.

The UPA regime has selected 90 districts and 5,000 minority dominated villages across the country for their supposed 'uplift', apart from working for schools and madrassas in these areas.

It is also talking about reservation to the community for their welfare. The government has adopted 25 recommendations of the Sachchar Commission, according to Zafar Ali Naqvi.[3]

The UPA government's move to constitute the Equal Opportunity Commission was another attempt to provide minorities reservation through the back door. The Minority Affairs minister told Parliament that the government is committed to establishing an EOC and is examining the recommendations of the expert group regarding its structure and functioning, a move that was opposed by several civil right groups, forcing the government to clarify the issue. The Minority Affairs minister argued that the government selected five schemes, for the welfare of the minorities under its 100-day agenda after the formation of UPA II. This is where the bone of contention lies. If the government is talking about equal opportunity, it has to be for all, not for any particular group. The pursuit of any policy of compartmentalization will lead only to alienation. Leaders like Arif Mohammed Khan have rightly opposed it saying: "If there is any clause that it is available to any particular group then it is wrong."[4]

The UPA is on the constant lookout for opportunities to build a basis to provide minority reservations, which India's Constitution does not permit. The Ranganath Mishra Commission report, tabled in Parliament in December 2009 recommends either giving a separate 10 per cent reservation for Muslims and 5 per cent for other minorities in government jobs or an 8.4 per cent reservation through the OBC quota. Salman Khurshid has said: "We are actively looking at the reservation issue."[5] The Congress favours giving reservation to minorities on the lines of quota structure already in place in Andhra Pradesh, Karnataka, Kerala and Tamil Nadu. These reservations are within the ambit of the 27 per cent of the OBC reservation. The very basis of reservation was questioned by the member-secretary of Ranganath Mishra Commission, Asha Das: "My basic objection was on identification, which is Chapter 7 of the report. I contended that the socio-economic condition of the people is not changing. As the list for the purpose was prepared for creative validity and suitability was taken into consideration, religion should have been considered. There are certain such examples such as Kudip Shri in Kerala and Velagu Syrle in Andhra, which follow the same method."

Another example where the government doles out financial largesse to Muslims is the Haj subsidy. The total Haj airline ticket subsidy was around Rs150 crore for the year 2001 and was earmarked to Rs 225 crore for 2005.[6] Effectively, the government doles out a subsidy of Rs 12,000 per haji![7] In 2007, the Haj subsidy paid by the Indian government was Rs 595 crore and for 2008, it had increased to Rs 700 crore. Since 1994, the round trip cost to Jeddah, Saudi Arabia has been fixed at Rs 12,000 per pilgrim, and the government foots the rest of the bill. In 2007, this difference came to Rs 47,454 per passenger.

The number of Haj pilgrims has risen significantly from 31,000 in 1995. In 2000, Air India carried 71,924 pilgrims to Jeddah and the Cabinet approved an increase in the total Haj pilgrims entitled to avail of the subsidy, to 1,23,211 from 1,10,000 a year earlier. According to sources, there are four main elements in calculating the cost of operating the Haj subsidy. These include ACMI (aircraft, crew, maintenance and insurance), other operational costs like airport charges and catering, unrecovered hidden cost like salaries of people working the whole year for smooth Haj operations and the service tax on Haj operations levied by the service tax department for which exemption has been denied by the Finance Ministry.

For giving a big push to some of its populist schemes, the Union Ministry of Minority Affairs will receive Rs 2,600 crore for the year 2010-2011. The Central Government in the National Budget presented in Lok Sabha, increased the allocation crore for the ministry by about Rs 850, which was earlier allotted Rs 1755 crore in the 2009-2010 budget. More than 90 per cent of the increased amount will go to three mega scholarship schemes and Multi-Sectoral Development Programmes.

There are certain problems with the leadership of the Muslim community. The leadership does not want its flock to see the light of development and wants them to remain backward, which is the reason modernization of Madrassa education is strongly opposed. The theocratic Muslim leadership still wants its people to remain glued to only theological education. The country has had three Muslim presidents, several chief ministers, Supreme Court judges and industrialists like Azim Premji. Such divisive policies as are being encouraged by the government now, far from benefitting the Muslims, will only generate animosity towards them in the long run. A secular country has to be administered only in a truly secular spirit, and all citizens of the country have equal right over its resources. This alone can promote peaceful coexistence. Someone has rightly said: "*Mussalmanon ke liye Hindustan se achcha desh aur Hinduon se achcha hamwatan koi nahin ho sakta*

(Muslims cannot hope for a country better than India and fellow-citizens better than Hindus)."

References

1. Ministry of Minority Welfare.
2. *Sahara Time*, 20 February 2010, p11
3. *Ibid*
4. *Sahara Time*, 22 August, p 47
5. *Sahara Time,* 14 August, p 32
6. http://indiabudget.nic.in/ub2005-06/eb/npe.pdf
7. *The Financial Express*, 13 September 2008

Rakesh Sinha is Associate Professor, Political Science, at Motilal Nehru College (E), Delhi University. A gold medalist and a topper of Delhi University, Sinha has authored biography of Dr K B Hedgewar, published by the Publication Division, Government of India in 2003, in five languages *Gurui* (Golwalkar) and *Indian Muslims*; *Political Journalism* (Rajanitik Patrakarita); *Deceptive Equality; Terrorism and Indian Media;* monograph: *Roti, Rozgar aur Rajya ka Sampradayikaran (A review of the Sachar Committee Report)* and intervention paper on Communal Violence Bill-2011.